Troubled Hearts, Troubled Minds

Making sense of the emotional dimension of learning

Peter Nelmes

Crown House Publishing Limited
www.crownhouse.co.uk

First published by
Crown House Publishing
Crown Buildings, Bancyfelin, Carmarthen, Wales, SA33 5ND, UK
www.crownhouse.co.uk

and

Crown House Publishing Company LLC
PO Box 2223, Williston, VT 05495, USA
www.crownhousepublishing.com

© Peter Nelmes, 2019

The right of Peter Nelmes to be identified as the author of this work has been asserted by him in accordance with the Copyright, Designs and Patents Act 1988.

Heart and brain image © SurfupVector and Arcady – fotolia.com

First published 2019.

All rights reserved. Except as permitted under current legislation no part of this work may be photocopied, stored in a retrieval system, published, performed in public, adapted, broadcast, transmitted, recorded or reproduced in any form or by any means, without the prior permission of the copyright owners. Enquiries should be addressed to Crown House Publishing.

The names of all the individuals mentioned in this book, and other identifying details, have been changed to ensure anonymity.

British Library of Cataloguing-in-Publication Data
A catalogue entry for this book is available from the British Library.

Print ISBN 978-178583410-3
Mobi ISBN 978-178583439-4
ePub ISBN 978-178583440-0
ePDF ISBN 978-178583441-7

LCCN 2019941876

Printed in the UK by
TJ International, Padstow, Cornwall

Contents

Introduction 1
    The concept at the heart of this book 4
    How this book is written 5
    Working with troubled children in the classroom 7
    The pervasiveness of underachievement 15
    Views of childhood 19
    The structure and language used in this book 21

**Part I: The construction and components of shared meanings:
    lessons from practice** 25

Chapter 1. The emotional component of teaching and learning 27
    An introduction to shared meanings 27
    Shared meanings, the emotions and teaching and learning 31
    Two case studies – Dean and Phil 43

Chapter 2. The teacher 53
    Becoming the teacher 53
    Establishing coherent meanings 59
    The concept of naughtiness as a barrier to coherence 65
    Disparity in adults' views 67
    Towards a coherent philosophy of childhood and its implications for
    the educator 76

Chapter 3. The context 79
    Acknowledging the power of the context 79

    The classroom and school environment 81
    Home experiences 82
    The past 85
Chapter 4. The learner 95
    Behaviour as a communication of unmet need 96
    Egocentricity 99
    Power, control and anxiety 101
    Structures and reference points – the foundations for learning 106
Chapter 5. Attuning to and containing emotions 113
    The less obvious roles of emotions in the classroom 113
    Containment 121

Part II: What does this mean for teachers? Lessons for practice 131

Chapter 6. How to talk to troubled children 133
    Modes of talk 133
    The art of de-escalation – tricks of the trade 139
    Checking that you are not the problem 142
    Teaching to the gaps 149
Chapter 7. Relf-regulation and supportive interventions 151
    The role of the internal monologue 152
    The nature of self-regulation 154
    The role of context in the creation of the internal monologue 156
    How to support the internal monologue of the troubled learner 158
    It all boils down to this 160
Conclusion 165
    We are all troubled 165
Bibliography 169

Introduction

For nearly 30 years I have worked in classrooms where the behaviour of the pupils has often been challenging, both in specialist provisions and in mainstream schools. I have witnessed probably more than my fair share of discord, strong words, strong emotions and flying objects. There have been times when the classroom felt like a place of chaos. And yet from the start of my career I felt drawn to this environment, despite the risks to my mental and, on occasion, physical health. Against the advice of my tutors during teacher training, who deemed such a choice *messy* or *career death*, I chose to work with the children who were the least suited to the rhythms of classroom life. This book describes the sense that I have since made of my experience.

Among the reasons for my career choice was the arrogance and idealism of youth. For reasons I can no longer recall, I reckoned I would be good at my job, and I wanted that job to be transforming children's lives. Within weeks of starting my first post, all sense of arrogance – and even competence – had gone. I was floored by the pace with which the mood in the classroom could change from peace to strife, from benevolence to naked hatred and aggression. These early experiences left me dazed and confused. All my beliefs, whether about myself or about teaching and learning, were lost. I realised that if I was going to survive, and possibly thrive, I needed to strip everything back and find a different way of thinking and acting.

One of the mistakes I made was thinking that the successes and failures in my lessons could be neatly ascribed to separate elements in the interaction. Successes were down to me, whereas failures were down to the children in front of me. This way of thinking was not sustainable, however. I knew that I was at least in part responsible when things went awry. As I slowly came to terms with the often chaotic world that I had chosen, I realised that there are in fact three components to my — and, indeed, to every — classroom, which each need to be taken into consideration: the pupils, the teacher and the context in which the teacher and the pupils meet, which includes everything from the weather outside, the physical attributes of the space, the type of school the classroom is in, and the practices and ethos of the wider society in which the school exists. This book is an anecdotal study of how I made sense of the many different ways in which these three components interact.

In time, I learned that none of these components can ever be isolated when looking at the success or failure of the classroom as a place of learning. This is not a commonly held view, if the labels that we ascribe to the children who are diverted from the educational mainstream into classrooms like mine are anything to go by. We used to define children with challenging behaviour by their inability to accommodate to us (for example, using the label 'maladjusted'), but we have thankfully retreated from such a stance of outright blame. We are now somewhat less harsh in our terms.

When I started teaching, my pupils were labelled as children with 'emotional and behavioural difficulties' (EBD), and this is the term I will use throughout the book, as the emotional and behavioural aspects are the focus of my exploration. Later on, the word 'social' was added to that epithet, and currently the recognised term is pupils with 'social, emotional and mental health difficulties'.[1] This move towards less-judgemental labelling is to be welcomed, but this book argues that none of these descriptors go far enough; we need a definition which locates the difficulty within the interaction between the pupil, the teacher and the context. As I learned very quickly, challenging behaviour is always contextual. At the start of my career, for example, the context of the children's most challenging behaviour was often my own classroom. The blame I directed at them for the horrendous lesson they had just had with me would be undermined when I heard them working harmoniously with the teacher in the neighbouring classroom in their next lesson. Clearly, and to my shame, the context and the teacher played a role.

---

1   Department of Education and Department for Health, *Special Educational Needs and Disability Code of Practice: 0 to 25 Years – Statutory Guidance for Organisations Which Work with and Support Children and Young People Who Have Special Educational Needs or Disabilities*. Ref: DFE-00205-2013 (January 2015). Available at: https://www.gov.uk/government/publications/send-code-of-practice-0-to-25, p. 98.

Another argument against these labels became clear as I understood that the children's challenging behaviour had a cause outside of their control. I learned that these behaviours never happened without understandable cause, and such a consideration makes any label which suggests that the difficulties are with the child seem misguided, if not insensitive. If a child came to school crying because they were being hit at home, we would not say that the problem was the crying but with the hitting. If the child replaces the crying with a different action, such as inattentiveness or impulsivity, the problem still remains the hitting. As is related in this book, this was something that took me time to learn.

There is yet another problem with the way in which children have been labelled during my time as a teacher, which is that although the children have been said to have both emotional and behavioural difficulties, it has clearly been the behavioural aspect which has prompted their removal from mainstream education. Children who are in emotional pain yet do not project that pain onto other people through aggression, damage or disruption have rarely made it through my classroom door. Perhaps this can help to explain why, for the first two thirds of my career, my clientele was at least 95% male. It seems that there was little ability or willingness to identify emotional problems in girls. I did not see children of either gender who had emotional problems but no behaviour problems, and I have never met a child with behaviour problems who did not have underlying emotional problems.

Therefore, when describing the children I have taught, I tend to use the term 'troubled children', to emphasise that for all that they *do* in the classroom or home – all the disruption or upset they may cause – they are still, by definition, mainly beings to whom something *is being or has been done*. This book is about how we can understand and teach all such children, not just the punchers, the kickers, the exploders, the flounce-off-ers, the chair-throwers and the otherwise actors-out. It is about how we can relate to any child who is troubled, howsoever they respond to that trouble. Any behaviour which impedes a child's learning and development needs to be understood and addressed, whether or not that behaviour is detrimental to the people around the child.

The concept at the heart of this book

Challenging behaviour, and how emotions affect the learning taking place (or not), is best understood by looking at the transaction between the teacher, the learner and the context in the classroom, and especially at what is created by the interaction between the three components. The concept at the heart of this book, therefore, is the product of this interaction: namely, shared meanings, those joint understandings that we create (or fail to). Examining this element of the process of teaching and learning can lead us to understand how emotions play a role in the learning of all children, and indeed adults, whether or not their behaviour is challenging, and whether or not they are troubled.

Shared meanings happen when two people think together, and can be represented pictorially thus:

The creation of shared meanings, I will show, is vital if teaching and learning is to take place. In order to fully understand how shared meanings work, we need to consider their emotional as well as cognitive dimensions. Education is, it is often said, about hearts and minds, but it seems to me that we have a lesser understanding of the role that the heart plays in learning. I set out to redress that imbalance, by explaining how hearts and minds – or emotion and cognition – work in a transactional relationship. If we fully understand this relationship, we become much more able to help troubled children to thrive and learn.

I explore shared meanings by describing the pupils I have met, what it has been like to be their teacher, and how context has played a role too. I interrogate the factors which promoted or hindered the meanings we tried to generate together. I first started to explore these factors with questions – such as, 'How can that boy be a right little sod for me and get so much praise for his work experience at the shop down the road?' When I had answered that question, other questions hove into view, and this book is testament to the journey (sometimes slow and often painful) towards enlightenment that I have been on. I aim to pass on the understandings I have come to in a way that can be taken and used as a model for anyone – be they teacher, other professional or, indeed, parent – who seeks to help troubled children and wants to understand how to help them learn.

This book is about unconventional people in unconventional classrooms. It is necessary, therefore, to do some scene setting before we get started. The rest of the introduction is devoted to this, beginning with a look at troubled children and the role of their teacher. Then it highlights the extent to which underachievement is so often a feature of these children's lives, before addressing you, the reader, by giving a brief warning about the content and language that you'll encounter as you read on. It also asks you to consider your own views of children and childhood, as this will inform your interpretation of the text. First, however, I explain why the unconventional nature of the subject matter necessitates an unconventional analysis.

How this book is written

The aim of this book is to present a theoretical concept that is firmly grounded in and illustrated by the nitty-gritty of practice, but I don't consider this to be a strictly academic text. I draw on stories involving many of the children whom I have taught over the years, which has some significant implications for how the book is written. I am writing about the meanings that I believe were made and shared in my classroom, and while I try to represent these children as fairly as possible, I am necessarily presenting my version of events. These stories are therefore partial in the sense that they can only present my interpretation. Also, if the meanings that are generated in my classroom are a result of the transactional relationship between myself, my pupils and the context in which we met, I clearly played an active part in creating these meanings as well as identifying and recording them. Thus I am aware that the stories I relate say much about me, as well as about the children whose behaviours and lives I describe.

Another reason why I cannot claim to adhere to the conventions of academic writing is that I need to be able to explore all the factors that influence the creation of shared meanings when two people interact. Interaction is rarely, if ever, a solely rational activity, even in everyday life, and it certainly was not in my classroom. As we shall see, there are many factors relating to the emotions that influence the nature of the meanings made, and these do not lend themselves easily to rational analysis. My pupils bring into the classroom things which seem, to me at least, to defy logical explanation; the classroom can often appear messy, confused, a place of dark feelings or high energy and exuberance. I need to be able to explore and, indeed, celebrate all of that, even if I cannot accurately measure the impact these factors have on the shared meanings made. The meanings that we have in our own heads are often multifactorial, ephemeral, easily lost and very difficult to describe with a sense of objectivity. The meanings we share with others are no different.

Therefore, this book cannot and does not strive for objectivity. That is not such a disadvantage as it may at first seem. We all have an ability to know when we make connections with other people and when we do not. We know when we have established a rapport with someone, and, equally, can tell when we are struggling to find common ground. I am relying on the creation of shared meanings being such a universal human experience that you, the reader, will know what I am talking about.

Another reason for this book's departure from traditional academic standards is that I cannot really define my terms. I do not want to get lost down the rabbit hole of trying to come up with a rational definition of the emotions, for example. I could spend chapters on such questions as 'How does an emotion differ from a mood?' or 'Is anger a true emotion if it is always a cover for something else, such as hurt or shame?' I want to be able to explore all that is connoted by the term *emotion*, from the feelings that come and go in an instant to our deeper yearnings which may only reveal themselves over the course of many years, and everything in between. Again, I am going to trust the reader's knowledge and intuition rather than spend time trying to rationalise that which is not wholly rational.

Introduction

Working with troubled children in the classroom

Who are these children?

As I have already mentioned, as soon as I started to teach troubled children, I realised that I had an inadequate understanding, both of my pupils and of what the process of teaching and learning was all about. It quickly became obvious that I needed to start paying attention to the emotions far more than I had assumed was necessary. For example, one of the first pupils I taught was Michael, a boy widely characterised by staff and pupils as a teenage thug. At 15 he was stocky and strong and feared by most of his classmates. He seemed to inhabit the role of school bully quite willingly. He took every chance available to sneer at his peers, denigrate them and, often, to hurt them physically. However, look beyond that behaviour and it was easy to see that in Michael's head, anxiety ruled. Michael feared lots of things, water especially. His mother once told me that he was scared to get into a bath, never mind lie back in it, even if she put less than an inch of water in it for him. Neither she nor I thought to question why she was still running his bath for him at 15 years of age. In almost all his activities he seemed frozen, incapable of vivacity, interest or even just making basic decisions.

So as I, his English teacher, approached the task of improving his writing abilities, I knew that he was not going to be able to write anything, because how could he start making decisions about which words to put down on paper? Like many of my pupils, Michael saw paper as an instrument of torture, a means by which one's shortcomings are turned into a permanent record. He would sit far away from my desk and well back from his own, his back against the wall both literally and metaphorically, his furrowed brow emanating threat, and his cheeks burning with shame and indignation. His hands would be balled tight, and there seemed little chance of getting them to pick up the pen. Even when he did, it seemed that deciding whether to use letters or digits to write the date was beyond him.

I used to write the beginning of the first sentence for him, in an effort to get him started. I narrated as I wrote. 'The match took place last Saturday morning when the weather was …' I would look at him and ask, 'So was the weather sunny or rainy?'

Michael would grunt, 'What? I dunno.'

I tried hard not to be cowed by the sense of sullen discomfort pulsing from across the desk.

'Come on, you were there. What was the weather like? Did it rain?'

Michael's gaze would sink down to the desk. If he did not engage now, he never would. I couldn't think what else to do. I had let him write about his favourite sport, cricket, even though the other pupils were writing fiction. I knew better than to ask him to be creative, an abhorrent activity in his view. He could simply report facts. All he had to do now was add the last word of the sentence. This is a 15-year-old boy, strangled with anxiety in the face of both his fears and his hopes. When the captain of Michael's local cricket club knocked on his door one Sunday morning, asking to speak to him because the first team was a player down and they wanted Michael to play for them – a dream scenario that Michael must have imagined many times – he refused to come out of his bedroom.

Michael was just one of many children to struggle to engage in my classroom because of their emotional state. Although there was a great deal of variety in the iterations of this struggle, I started to become aware that these children did have some things in common. Cooper, Smith and Upton's list of commonalities between children who have been excluded from the classroom or school resonated with my own experience.[2] It describes a life of underachievement at school, with few or no friends. Engagement in school is characterised by behavioural problems. Family life is often marked by trauma, abuse and violence. Social care is often involved. Low self-esteem is cited as a common factor, and I would also cite a sense of shame.

My thinking about these children started to gain some coherence, despite the frenetic, chaotic nature of my lessons, and despite the myths that circulated in the staffrooms of schools like mine. 'You should only teach EBD for seven years or you'll burn out' was a regularly uttered axiom. Another was that the children were either *mad, bad or sad.* This description, I soon realised, was unhelpful. Perhaps it was a form of self-protection, a way of keeping a distance between

---

[2] Paul Cooper, Colin J. Smith and Graham Upton, *Emotional and Behavioural Difficulties: Theory to Practice* (Abingdon and New York: Routledge, 1994).

the speaker and the subject. By using a judgement or a label one could impose a meaning on the child, rather than construct a meaning with them, which might expose the speaker to the child's pain. And it seemed to me that these children were the unluckiest of the unlucky. Their backgrounds often featured combinations of negative factors that multiplied their misery exponentially. Children, for example, whose trauma in their early years had led them to be removed from their families, only to be put with foster parents who did not want, or were not able, to care about them.

I believe that I have never met a child who is intrinsically so disturbed as to warrant the descriptor 'mad'. I have never met a child who is intrinsically 'bad', although I have seen children do things to others which are appallingly hurtful or cruel. These actions always have reasons which at least explain if not pardon them. And as for the word 'sad', well, while it fits, such a small word cannot really do justice to the misery and challenge in these children's lives. I have never met a child whose challenging behaviour did not have a recognisable root cause, and perhaps *sad* is the best catch-all term for such roots, even if it does not communicate the depths of the problems that many of my pupils faced.

I have my own definition of what I mean by troubled children: they are people with a greater than average need to communicate and a smaller than average ability to do so. In other words, they come into the classroom needing to create shared meanings more than anyone else because they are lost and lonely, but they find this much more difficult than the majority of their peers do.

They usually arrive at school with paperwork describing some of the sadness that they have experienced. Incident reports from primary school, exclusion letters, safeguarding concerns, social services interventions, records of entries into and exits from a much higher than average number of schools. This all speaks of rejection, failure and probable disaffection. But the paperwork just records the chapter headings of their misery. It does not capture all the sentences in between or the day-to-day nature of their plight. Perhaps the most cogent understanding of their sadness comes from the feeling that you may get after spending even 15 minutes in their company. Your head may be filled with difficult feelings – such as anxiety, irritation or hurt – and it is a relief when you can get away from them. You may think, 'My word! That was hard work, and somewhat unpleasant.' You go off and, to regain your sense of well-being, find someone you can connect positively with – your friends, colleagues you like or your family.

But what does the troubled child do? Often they go on to reproduce those same negative feelings in the next interaction they have, and the next, and so on *ad nauseam*. Their ability to connect with other people is often severely impaired or skewed, and so they end up being marginalised by the rest of us. They are the children educated in the corridor because their presence in the classroom causes too many problems. They are the children who never get asked back for play dates or parties, or who get passed from one foster carer to another. They are vulnerability hiding in plain sight. Their dilemma is acute; they cannot live with people, nor can they live without them. Even though they may appear wildly antisocial, most of them abhor isolation. As a teacher, I soon learned that isolation could not, and indeed should never, be enforced upon them. They will fight it with all their will. They cannot be alone. Their hearts drive them again and again into the very interactions they struggle with. They are like incompetent gamblers, who – despite a lifetime of losing – feel compelled to come back to the table to roll the dice one more time, squeezing yet another final drop of hope from an almost empty reserve.

The role of the teacher of troubled children

There are many aspects to teaching troubled children and these are detailed throughout the book. For now, I just want to highlight some of the particulars, to give a flavour of what the job entails. Trying to interact and make meanings with children whose lives have so much trauma, loss and hurt in them is not easy. It's even harder when they are not sitting calmly and telling you about their misery, but instead are manifesting it by telling you to *fuck off* or by throwing punches at their neighbour. Making sense of the role, and above all making sense with the children, necessitates the recognition that the role is not a wholly rational or conventional one. For example, I have never had the luxury, as teachers in other areas of the profession sometimes have, of being able to decide, as I plan my lesson, what meanings are going to be made when I deliver it to the class. The children in front of me were never going to look up eagerly at me, waiting to catch every pearl of wisdom I cast their way, and receive my lesson exactly as I had intended it to be received.

After perhaps a rather shameful number of mistakes, I learned that the teacher of troubled children needs to possess and practise certain basic skills and attributes:

An acute awareness of the level and nature of the pupils' understanding of any subject

You have an extremely narrow window through which to connect with your pupils, academically speaking. You have to judge the size and shape of their current understanding. If your lesson is too easy, they will not learn anything, they will be bored, and they will kick off as a result. A smidgeon too hard and they will kick off as a result. Also, lessons have to be fun and immediately engaging. This is before you take the emotional dimensions of the activity into consideration.

Differentiate between meanings and words

You need to be aware that just because you have said something does not mean it has been listened to. Telling does not equal being told. Your words are rarely taken at face value. It is important for you to be circumspect about the words they use too. One of the mantras that has stuck with me throughout my career is, 'Pay attention to what they do, not what they say they are going to do.' And the reason for that is because behaviour is not just a form of communication, but is often a more honest form of communication than the spoken word. But even that needs a good deal of interpretation sometimes. Recently one pupil, Shaun, was asked to discuss his recent aggression towards some other children with me and a colleague. His first reaction was denial and flight. 'I'm sick of being accused of things I haven't done, and I'm sick of all you lot in this shitty school. I might as well just take off. In fact, that is what I am going to do, right now!' And in so saying he marches to the main doors and then fades to the right, standing halfway down the corridor, still swearing that we have seen the last of him even though he is in full view.

Be prepared to interpret everything

Shaun's talk is easy to see through, as long as you don't react to it and push him into carrying out his threat. No matter how much he protests, the conviction is not there in his voice. What he is saying is a pretty poor indicator of what is going on inside. But his actions are only marginally more helpful. In fact, in order to make sense of Shaun, and his seemingly incessant need to hit and hurt, a great deal of skilful interpretation is needed, but it is possible, nonetheless.

Respect for the pupil's 'voice' is not always appropriate

It would be lovely if every interaction with my pupils could be reciprocal and facilitative, but there are times when I need to take control over the whole process. This raises two risks. One is that your interpretation is rejected because the pupil has no sense of ownership ('You're not being fair, you're just picking on me!'), and the second, perhaps greater, danger is that you come close to playing a god-like role in their lives. But the need to step in is so great that to not do so would be a form of neglect. For example, with a class of 12 troubled and potentially troubling children, there are of course times when I have had no choice but to prohibit certain opinions and actions. Everyone must keep their language respectful of others, for example.

I have to do what I believe is best, even if the child is in disagreement with my actions following a contravention, and strife may occur as a result. It's worth the battle, because if I allow disrespect in my classroom then greater strife will ensue. Another obvious example is if there is a safeguarding concern and the child does not want what they have said to be reported. In such cases, the adults have to take over and act in the best interest of the child, regardless of their wishes.

The problems really start in less clear-cut situations. The children I teach occasionally seem so lost in their lives that it seems wrong not to step in and sort things out for them. Malky, for example, is a boy who is relentlessly cheery, who walks down the corridor demanding high fives from everyone, even staff who have their hands full of papers or equipment. The high fives are way too hard, and sting, but Malky just laughs when he is told this. His cheeriness grates on me, I have to admit. It is difficult to guide him away from this high-octane bonhomie thing that he has going on. It is not just the high fives, it is the sneaking up behind people and making them jump, and the constant commentary on himself and how he is a prankster, a laugh-a-minute guy, and even, as he simply throws a ball from one hand to the other, a magician. ('How is that magic, Malky?' 'It just is. Hee hee, I'm so funny!') I once asked him whether other people might see things differently, and whether, for instance, when he did the old trick of pointing to a pretend mark on a classmate's chest and when they looked down, brought his hand up to catch them on the nose, they might not call him a *laughmeister* but a *pain in the neck*.

I should have behaved better, it is true. I cannot in all conscience *not* begin to challenge his attempts to frame all his interactions in the way that he seems to want to do so, but I need to be more professional than I was then. I know there are times when I can see the flipside of his enthusiasm for terrible jokes, when he looks exhausted and depressed. I know enough about his chaotic home life – and his worries about his ballooning weight and his problem with body odour – to see that here is a boy in serious need of help.

On one occasion Malky angered a much older boy with one of his 'pranks' and I had to physically prevent this boy from entering the corridor in order to hurt Malky. When the older boy calmed down he said, 'Thank you for standing in my way.' This is part of what the job entails – standing in their way, acknowledging that even if you don't know what is best for the child, the little you do know is a hell of a lot better than whatever wisdom sent them down the path they are currently on. When I first started this work, I thought that everyone had a right to have their voice heard, and that I was in no position to judge, or to say how to live a better life. It turns out, however, that as young and inexperienced as I was, I had a much better idea than the Malkys of the world did, and if I did not intervene in their lives, then they would get beaten up regularly, or fail to make any friends because of their manner or their smell, and I would be failing in my duty towards them. With pupils like Malky there is a pressure to intervene, to act because you believe that you 'know best', even though such interventions feel uncomfortable in their one-sidedness.

Have faith in the child and in all children

I need to act for children like Malky because to not do so would feel neglectful. It would seem like leaving him to a fate he does not deserve. Malky needs someone to show him that there is a better way to be living his life. If I can see how Malky might benefit from making changes, then I am obliged to act. I need to be aware that I am aiming to work *with* Malky rather than *for* him or, worse, *on* him. Even if our relationship is heavily asymmetrical there needs to be some feeling of a move towards democracy and reciprocity, at least. So as I reframe some of his actions (such as his pranks) as not funny but irritating, rather than dismiss them, I can help Malky to see what his intentions are – and if they are to initiate interaction and friendship, to see that there are better ways of achieving this.

Such an approach involves a journey based on faith. I need to have faith in Malky; he is not inherently irritating or malicious, but a good person who has lost his way a bit. I need to have faith that there is a better life for him. I need to have faith in myself too. I need to believe that what I am doing is not damaging Malky. I don't want to make his life worse in a botched attempt to help. He does not want someone to lift the lid too much on his feelings, so that he is forced to face issues that he is not ready for. Neither does he want someone to sympathise with him, a bleeding heart who frames his life as a tragedy that he cannot do much about. He probably needs someone who can gently and supportively insist that he tries to be friendlier and gets a wash a bit more often, and who does not get too upset if Malky hits out a little in the process of taking the message on board, allowing him to save face with a weak excuse or two along the way. I do not know how Malky would react to someone speaking to him in a way that insists upon the reality of the situation, because every child is different, but I suspect that he might respond positively to someone making a genuine connection with him for what might be the first time in a while, even if he is unable to acknowledge it there and then.

Be prepared to take on other roles

Unless you act as relationship counsellor, you probably won't get any teaching done for the first hour after break or lunchtime. Similarly, you need to be part social worker, police officer, life coach and foster parent, just to get the children into a state where they may be ready to learn, so you can start to teach.

Learn as much as you can

You need to know about attachment theory, attention deficit hyperactivity disorder (ADHD), pathological demand avoidance syndrome, foetal alcohol syndrome, dyslexia, dyspraxia, autism, anxiety, depression, psychosis, sexualised behaviours, obsessive compulsive disorder, the impact of domestic violence, drug abuse, alcoholism, and so on. Read as widely as you can and ask any other professionals who are working with the child for advice.

But accept that this learning may count for little with the next child through your classroom door

They may have several labels, but you are dealing with a child, not a diagnosis, and they will be different from any other child you have met before. To paraphrase Tolstoy, each unhappy child will be unhappy in their own way, and the variety is astonishing and fascinating.

The pervasiveness of underachievement

Cooper, Smith and Upton's list of common attributes of troubled children, cited previously, includes underachievement. Of course, this issue is problematic in any school, but I want to stress the extent to which this is a factor for troubled children. It is difficult to convey the degree of underachievement that can be involved. For understandable reasons it is a sensitive subject; it seems like a harsh judgement to describe troubled children as virtually unable to learn, but that is what many of them are. When I first got a job working with children labelled as having EBD, I wondered why nobody had mentioned their learning difficulties, as it seemed that the two were inexorably linked. Sinason talks of the stupidity or stupefaction that comes with grief, and this chimes with my experience of these children, in that there often seems to be a very close relationship between experience of emotional difficulty and a significantly reduced capacity to learn.[3]

I became aware of the phenomenon of underachievement on my first day as a newly qualified teacher. I asked my manager to comment on my lesson plans for the day. I was teaching geography to a group of 15-year-olds in a unit for excluded children. My manager looked at the plan and said, 'This is the plan for the entire half term, right?' Further evidence of my need to adjust my expectations came when I got into the first lesson. It took me a while to realise that the outline map of the world which I had handed out to each pupil had little or no meaning to them. Some of them had it upside down, and I do not think any of them could distinguish that the lines represented the borders between countries and between land and water. When I started to pick out places that I thought they would know, I realised that they had no idea which were countries and which were cities; indeed, they did not seem to have a clear understanding of these concepts.

Despite their underachievement I felt strongly that my pupils did not have specific diagnosable learning difficulties; they were just sad. It was their unhappiness that meant they were so often unable to take anything from any lesson they attended. Learning should be exponential – the more you learn, the more you are able to learn. But my pupils seemed stuck at square one, and so they fell way, way behind their mainstream peers. This then brings further problems, as they start to become conscious of their own limitations, and they enter into a vicious cycle of shame and disaffection, leading to further underachievement.

Once I had got a reasonable handle on behaviour management, I learned to combine hyper-vigilance with inner calmness. I developed the art of thinking through the pupils' problems with engagement in class activities even before they realised there was a problem. These skills gave me some breathing space, and I could then concentrate on trying to understand how and why our emotions affect the way in which we learn. Intuitively we may know that happy people are going to thrive and learn better than unhappy people are, but why is this the case? Why do so many children whose lives are marked by tragedy of some kind then have this compounded by losing the drive and the capacity to learn? They have nearly two

---

3   Valerie Sinason, *Mental Handicap and the Human Condition: An Analytic Approach to Intellectual Disability*, 2nd edn (London: Free Association Books, 2010).

decades to get ready for adulthood, and to practise learning, so why do they not become adept at it?

Even in the dark, chaotic days at the start of my career, this question held me in its thrall. What if there is a direct link between emotional development and cognitive development? What would that look like? What would that mean for my teaching? What does that mean for the children in front of me? Furthermore, what does it mean for the rest of us and for how we live our lives?

As I overcame my own shortcomings and insecurities as a teacher, I noticed that there were very few people out there with an answer to the question I was wrestling with. It took a while for me to realise how many of my colleagues were on the point of collapse through stress – victims of the attrition that took place in their classrooms day after day – and I realised that the shame of not being able to teach, of not being able to get their pupils to learn, was a significant factor in this stress. And even those teachers who were really good at classroom management appeared to accept without too many questions the very slow rate at which the children were learning. They did not have a choice but to work with what was in front of them, and the children in front of them brought all sorts of barriers to learning into the classroom interaction.

As time went on, I started to see trends – small parts of the overall puzzle. I could see a link between low self-esteem and perfectionism, for example, in pupils such as Andrew, who always refused to draft his work, and who began each writing task with renewed enthusiasm and great care, only to rip his work up in a terrible black tantrum at the first error. I could see that his low self-esteem meant that only brilliance and perfection would tip him into the positive; anything short of that was failure. Once I had recognised this in Andrew, I started to see different manifestations of the same phenomenon in others.

I could also see that some pupils were more comfortable with failure than with success. Success was scary because you could not be sure what it would lead to. I could also see that a very common characteristic, even among the supposedly streetwise adolescents, was an egocentricity that, chronologically at least, they should have left behind years ago. I understood that they needed early childhood experiences dressed up as teenage-appropriate activities. One boy, Terry, who was 17 and whose arm featured a large tattoo (unfinished because it was too painful to complete) wanted only to read the Mr Men books by Roger Hargreaves.

Then there were children for whom the classroom was merely a forum in which to act out – or re-enact – psychological games, attention-seeking ploys or attempts to provoke rejection from the adults. And, as I have mentioned, there was the spectre of disaffection, draining the life out of the classroom. These children did not seem to be like those individuals who have taken a knock, or even a kicking, and who are now struggling to get back on their feet. They seemed to have a whole different set of beliefs and customs. They inhabited a different country to the one in which I thought all children lived. These pupils lived in a world where people knew but did not admit that learning did not really happen. It was a world of loneliness and shame. It often felt as though they believed that events in the other, real world – and the ways in which people there were successful – had very little to do with them or their lives.

Each one of the hundreds of children I saw over the years added to my conviction that there was something there to be made sense of, something for which my training had left me unprepared, and of which I remained ignorant. During my year-long teacher training course we only spent a few afternoons on behaviour management, but even that was misguided because it presented challenging behaviour as a thing in and of itself, rather than as the consequence of the child's unmet needs. The idea that experiencing trauma of some kind might slow or extinguish one's capacity to learn was not broached at all.

I spent some time in those early days thinking not just that I was not a good teacher, but that I was not a teacher at all. What was I supposed to do when my knowledge of how to teach reading did not cover sitting with a child who could decode perfectly but could not remember the start of the sentence they were reading by the time they got to its end, and so never made any sense of the words? Or a child who could not read because they always looked at anywhere on the page other than where the words were?

Two and a half decades later, I find myself now in possession of a largely coherent theory, an answer to the question about what is really going on in classrooms where there is – depending on your point of view – either disobedience, challenging behaviour, sad or anxious children, or teachers who are not connecting with their pupils. I mention these alternative views because there was one niggling thought that I had throughout those early days. I had to consider that the mirror image of their failure to learn was my failure to teach, and how could I be sure that the problem was not mine?

Views of childhood

Working with troubled children forces you to confront the concept of shame. It comes at you from several angles and, unless you deal with it, it can eat you up. Firstly, there is the shame that exists because the learners are not learning in the way that they should, and therefore the teacher is not teaching in the way that they should. Secondly, there is the shame that follows all the discord, aggression and cruelty that is enacted both in the classroom and, by some of the pupils, later in their lives. It is hard to bear witness to actions that hurt and destroy and not feel that, in some way, you have been part of those actions. Also, my job offers a clear window onto the darker side of what it is to be human. When I tell strangers what I do, the response is often, 'That must be so rewarding.' The sanitised view of special educational needs that lies behind such a statement does not come close to embracing all the disturbance, violence and often insurmountable tragedy in these young lives.

Perhaps some people do not want to embrace this violence, disturbance and tragedy. Perhaps they do not want to acknowledge that there is a dark side to being human. They do not want to see it in others or in themselves. Perhaps this is why the same attention, resources or social acceptance afforded to people with physical needs is not usually given to those of us with emotional needs. Learning difficulties, for example, are categorised by degree of severity and the nature of the difficulty presented. We have no such refinements for EBD. On a broader level, children with EBD have not, it could be argued, been included in the move towards greater inclusivity. The feelings they may induce in those around them makes their inclusion in public life far from straightforward. We accept, for example, that a cinema needs to be accessible to a child with a physical disability, but sitting next to a child whose emotional needs mean they have poorly regulated behaviour and poor social skills, and who not only rustles their sweet wrappers but insults you when you ask them to stop, is a different matter. This book focuses on the children who would typically make undesirable neighbours in the cinema.

I feel that it is important to be accurate in my descriptions of what the pupils in my classroom did, and what they still get up to. If I see a story in the local paper about aggravated burglary, death by dangerous driving or another heinous crime, I half expect the perpetrator to be an ex-pupil of mine. Even when I understand the reasons for their behaviour, my pupils are often still difficult to be with. Most of us have or have had contact with one or two people who act in ways we cannot understand, and which pose a risk to our well-being or that of those we love. We might reduce the time we spend with them as much as possible, because we have not got the energy or resources to deal with them. There are enough problems in our lives without going looking for more. We all have a cut-off point in this respect. My pupils largely fall into the category of people who others want to avoid. But they are still children, even when they are taller than us, spotty and loud, and even when their actions are damaging to those around them. They still deserve to be understood, and they still deserve an education.

It is easy to sympathise with these children while reading the stories I tell about them; they all have backstories that will make most people feel like weeping. However, it needs to be said that readers who simply take the side of the children described herein are, to some degree, missing the point. They are also the very individuals who are avoided, shunned and judged to be wanting by most of society, most of the time. And there is no denying that there is good reason for this. So, I would ask you to be aware that these children are easier to like on paper than they are when you are actually with them. Even if you are a skilled handler of unruly children – and are able to bring out the best in them – they are still hard to be with, and your emotional reservoir will eventually drain empty if you stay with them for too long.

I am not trying to induce in the reader any romantic notions of these children. I have not spent my years as their teacher simply marvelling at their nobility and dignity, their resourcefulness and courage. It has been, at times, very hard to live with day after day of their squabbling, selfishness, petty thuggery and mess. Sometimes all I want from them is just a little bit of instant compliance, even on such a small issue as putting the tops back on the felt tip pens when they have finished with them, or returning a pass when kicking around a football. It is wearisome when such compliance almost never comes. But I am also aware that many of these children live with a weight of sadness that I never experienced in my childhood.

I am desperate for compliance partly for selfish reasons, of course; life is easier when there is less strife at each turn and with each interaction. But there is a more compelling reason. It does not take much imagination to look at the trajectory of these children's lives and find cause for great concern. They have futures with a greater likelihood of trouble ahead, including marital breakdown, drug abuse, unemployment and mental ill health.[4]

So, how are we to view these children? I have often wondered about their nature as a group as they have sworn, hit, spat, cried and stomped around my classroom. Are they the weakest of the weak, without backbone, resilience or resolve (which is how I have heard them judged)? Or are they in fact children who – no matter how much life has battered them with misfortune, loss, neglect and trauma – refuse to go quietly into the abyss, and whose humanity cries out against the cruel gods in whose charge they have fared so badly? I will leave that for the reader to decide, but I would argue one final point on the matter. These children are no different from any other except in the circumstances of their lives. Like any child, their development is down to an interplay between nature and nurture. The fact that this interplay has for them led to perhaps extreme behaviours should not trick us into seeing them as being different to any other child. Their developmental path may be more meandering and more challenging than the paths of most other children, but they should not be treated as different animals.

The structure and language used in this book

The book is divided into two parts: the first comprising lessons from practice and the second looking towards a coherent theory that can then inform practice. As a continuation of the scene setting, Chapter 1 explores the emotional background of teaching and learning, and the nature of shared meanings. As I have

---

4 Cooper, Smith and Upton, *Emotional and Behavioural Difficulties*.

mentioned, there are three components of shared meanings in the classroom: Chapter 2 looks at the teacher and Chapter 3 at the role of context, while Chapter 4 focuses on the learner. These chapters explore the lessons that I have learned from practice. The separation of the three components is useful for the purposes of structuring the book, but is actually misleading because of the transactional nature of the relationship between them. Just as it is impossible to have teaching without learning, so it is impossible to describe the teacher without considering their learners, and vice versa. There is, therefore, considerable conceptual overlap between these three chapters. Chapter 5 then considers what it means to attune to the emotional dimension of classroom interactions.

After Chapter 5 there is a slight change of direction, in that I move towards a more coherent theory and put greater emphasis on the lessons for practice. Chapter 6 explores the best modes of talk to use when teaching troubled children. Chapter 7 presents a way of conceptualising all that has been described in the book into a simple theoretical model. I conclude with reflections on our relationship with these children on a societal level.

As I have said, I wish to be accurate in my portrayal of my pupils and my interactions with them, and the language of the book reflects that desire. Not all the children who passed through my door succeeded in improving their learning or in holding their lives together. Some failed, some were failed by us. The phrase that I came back to again and again was that there was a 'mountain of misery' out there, and I had to be content with dealing with as much as I could, even if my efforts made only a small difference to the overall size of the mountain. I learned that the most professional approach was to try my hardest for each child, but not to sacrifice my energies, my emotions or my self-esteem on children who, despite our best efforts and through no fault of their own, were unable to access our support. Readers need to be aware that some of the stories in this book have upsetting endings or include descriptions of actions that make for uneasy reading.

I do not try to sugar-coat any of the children's actions, or my emotions and opinions. Some of the children were painful to be with at times and it is important, I feel, to convey the nature of the difficulties we faced. There were times when some of the children acted in ways that were deeply disturbing. Again, I need to recognise this and report it faithfully. Some of these children had experienced disturbing brutality and so reflected that in the actions they took.

There have been times when I have seen parents or other people in the children's lives in distress. For example, if a child's behaviour stems from the fact that there was violence in the home, it is likely there were other victims in that home too. In practice there may have been a great deal of support going into the house from a wide range of professionals, but to describe such support (where it happened – it was not always the case) is beyond the remit of this book. I consider simply the child's needs, and this may seem somewhat callous at times. Therefore, the book comes with a warning that at times the reading is not easy. Please be aware as you continue.

Part I
The construction and components of shared meanings: lessons from practice

Chapter 1

The emotional component of teaching and learning

An introduction to shared meanings

Central to this book is the premise that shared meanings are vital for teaching and learning.

It's human nature to seek to connect with other people, and shared meanings help us to feel close to others, shape our friendships and give us a sense of connection to the important people in our lives. They also have another function. They are the means by which we transfer information, understandings and skills. They are the vehicle for teaching and learning. As such, they fulfil perhaps our two greatest needs: to connect with others and to learn. Teaching and learning is an attempt to control the generation of shared meanings by introducing a sense of formality, so that the transfer of knowledge and skills is maximised.

There are several features of shared meanings that are important to point out before we examine in greater detail their role in teaching and learning.

We know when shared meanings are being generated

We know what it is to be able to look into someone's eyes and know that they are connected to us. Sharing the same joke, thought or feeling is a common experience. Equally, we know when someone is not truly attending to us, or when we are trying to get our point across but failing to do so. The children I have worked with are no different in that they seek this connection. Some of them may seek out connection with others in strange ways. Some, for example, seem to feel that their only route is through antagonising others, but the need for connection is still the primary driver for their behaviour.

The ability to connect with others can grow or fade

Many of my pupils had got used to living in a way that does not involve rich connections with other people, and the worry is that this becomes the norm for them as they grow into adulthood. Shaun seemed to be on such a path. When I met him, he was 13, and he seemed determined to go out of his way to be mean and create upset in others. We knew that his home life was chaotic and that he was a product of neglect, so we flooded his life with kindness, and occasionally he showed signs of wanting to interact in positive ways, during which both he and his interlocutors felt happy.

But all our behaviour management techniques failed to work. We put him on internal work experience, for example, helping out in a class of much younger pupils, which he loved. We allowed him to help the school caretaker, because he was good with his hands. We fixed up a range of rewards that really motivated him. Above all, we caught him being good and that changed his image around the school. But our attempts to make him feel valued never really managed to change his image of himself. I did some home visits, only to find that his dad was as immature as him, competing with his son to get my attention, in a way that made it no surprise when Shaun came in the day after and reported that his dad had said I was stupid. It seemed to be part of the family ethos to belittle everyone.

We continued to try to be as positive as possible. Shaun often talked of how thick he was, even though his reading and writing were way ahead of the rest of his class. He often talked about how ugly and fat he was, though he was really quite slim. 'I'm obeast!' he would say and there was no gainsaying him. Shaun was negative not just in his talk but in his actions. If he was playing with building bricks, he would get to the point when the bricks he had been putting together risked resembling something – a house, a car or maybe just a wall. The first few times when I made the mistake of commenting that his creation could be something, Shaun would instantly destroy it. Then he internalised this conversation for himself and regularly started to build something, only to rapidly destroy it when any pattern or potential in his creation became apparent.

His classmates hated and feared him. They had no understanding of him beyond his frequent cruelty. They saw his identity as purely negative, despite their incredible levels of tolerance and kindness shown over the years – it was hard for them to see anything else. Whenever there was any interaction in a lesson – such as a debate, a conversation or just a request for a show of hands – Shaun would instantly switch off, and as likely as not disrupt the forum with silly noises or another favourite saying – 'This is shit!' – and prepare himself to meet the inevitable challenge from staff with even more obduracy and the closing statement of 'I don't care.'

Shaun seemed to be heading for a future with little chance of rich connections with others. When he was 18 and about to leave us, we reminisced about the year in which we first met, when he had often run around the school with two other boys, just for the hell of it. 'Those days,' he said, 'they were the best.'

In the months before he left, he turned his negativity inward. It seemed as though he realised that the process of leaving us meant that we were not a valid repository for all his difficult feelings any more. I worry about Shaun's future. I hope that he can find the ability to connect with others, and not become someone who floods their interactions with their own thoughts and feelings to the extent that there is no room for those of their interlocutor.

Shared meanings are generated by words plus context

Shared meanings are not the same as words alone. Therefore, they are difficult to control, and can be ephemeral and easily lost. As I said in the introduction, we cannot be sure that the words we say will equate to the meanings generated. Shared meanings are created by more than one person: there is a reciprocity involved, a degree of back and forth. This reciprocity might take the form of a discussion – checking what each other is saying and getting from the interaction – but sometimes it might just be a look.

As such, meanings can change in an instant. You can feel that you are really seeing eye to eye with someone and then an action or word can cause the feeling to evaporate. For example, I once taught a group of lads *Romeo and Juliet*, and we had lots of fun acting out a fight scene, using the language from the text. It felt like a really successful activity. Then I finished the lesson with some incredibly beautiful music that I felt really captured the tragedy of the story. All the boys just started laughing uncontrollably at what they saw as the dreariness of the singing. I was so disappointed, and not a little embarrassed, because I was so sure that they would see the music in the same way I did. Personal meanings may be relatively straightforward, but shared meanings can easily escape us.

Context can make the meanings of words difficult to control, but it is not as if we use words logically anyway. If you think that words are the tool of perfect logic, spending time with children whose autism has accentuated their sense of literalness will convince you otherwise. For example, Geoffrey, who can forget to think about other people's feelings when he interacts with them, and so can seem malicious and aggressive. On one occasion, I catch him giving a girl 'birthday beats', by which I mean he is punching her on the arm, one punch for each year she is old. I stop him, and he asks why I have done so. I tell him to look at the girl's face. He sees the tears streaming down and says, 'Oh, I see what you mean.'

Later I tell him that it upsets me to see him doing unkind things to his friends.

'Why?' asks Geoffrey.

'Well, *for one thing* I don't think you really enjoy it overall, because you are always sad about it afterwards, when you realise that your friend is now sad,' I say. And then I suggest that we should get him back into class so he can apologise to the girl. I start walking but I notice that Geoffrey is not with me. I ask him to come along but he refuses. His shoulders have tensed again. I walk back and say, 'Geoffrey, come on. Let's get you back to class.'

'But I want to know.'

'You want to know what?'

'I want to know the other things. You said, "for one thing," so there must be others. I want to know what they are.'

Shared meanings are at the heart of all we do to help learners

I have worked alongside a range of different play, art and music therapists, psychodynamic therapists, and clinical and educational psychologists. Attuning to the children, understanding how they can collaborate to produce shared meanings, is the goal of all these professionals in their respective roles. Similarly, in school, our approach does not differ if the child is emotionally troubled, if they have autism, severe learning difficulties or a specific learning difficulty, such as ADHD. The physical implementation of the strategies may differ, but the aims in each case are the same: maximise the shared meaning between the child and the people around them.

Shared meanings, the emotions and teaching and learning

I'll now try to explain the process of teaching and learning to show the centrality of shared meanings, and the role of the emotions too. Let us start with the idea that the interaction between the teacher and learner is simply academic, cognitive or rational. Even within these narrow parameters, which ignore the richness of most human interactions, the idea of shared meaning is key because at the heart of the teaching and learning process is the point at which the teacher meets the learner, and at which their two minds overlap.

This overlap is crucial, and teachers work hard to shape how it happens. Simply put, if the teacher's talk is too complex – beyond the learner's current level of understanding of a topic – it is going to make no sense to the learner, who will therefore not learn anything. If the teacher makes things too easy, then the meaning that the teacher and learner make together will not extend the learner or introduce them to new ways of understanding. So it is important that the teacher accurately assesses the learner's current levels of understanding, so that they can pitch the complexity of the lesson just ahead of that understanding. Once the teacher can structure this new meaning in such a way that the learner can make sense of it for themselves, the learner's understanding is taken forward. This is Vygotsky's zone of proximal development.[1]

In the simple example below, in an art lesson, the teacher sees that the learner can draw circles.

The teacher thinks that he can extend the learner's drawing skills. Perhaps he knows that the learner likes trains, and so uses that as motivation (although talk of motivation is letting the emotions creep into our example a little, of course). 'Hey,' says the teacher, 'if you know how to draw a reasonably accurate circle, I can show you how to draw a train.'

---

1   Jerome Bruner, Vygotsky: A Historical and Conceptual Perspective. In James V. Wertsch (ed.), *Culture, Communication, and Cognition: Vygotskian Perspectives* (Cambridge: Cambridge University Press, 1985), pp. 21–34.

'Okay,' the pupil says, and has a go at following the teacher's demonstration but struggles.

So the teacher, refining his understanding of the learner's ability, decides to make the instructions more easily understandable for the pupil. He breaks them down into steps and provides a commentary to help the learner think the steps through.

'Step one is to draw a circle. Then draw another one of the same size. Then draw two lines connecting the circles. Next, rub out one part of one circle, and then you have a cylinder.'

The teacher can see that they are both on the same page in their thinking now. There is a perfect match between the two of them, a reciprocity in their understanding. With the teacher's guidance, the pupil can do something he has never been able to do before, i.e. begin to draw a train.

Then the teacher goes away. The pupil is left to go through the steps on his own. He remembers the way that the teacher talked the problem through, and showed him how to break it down into steps. He remembers what to focus his attention on, and the script needed to get him started. Perhaps the learner repeats the conversation that he had with the teacher, but on his own this time. It might help to say it out loud at first, so that he can use his auditory memory to help his

The emotional component of teaching and learning

cognition. He might say something like, 'So we start by drawing a cylinder, which is just two similar-sized circles connected by straight lines. And then I have to rub something out? Oh yes, I remember.'

In this case, the learner has internalised the dialogue between himself and the teacher for the first four steps only. He can't quite get the fifth or sixth step, so he will need some more help from the teacher; they will have to create the shared meaning again to support the learner's internal monologue until he can appropriate all the steps for himself. But that's okay, practice makes perfect. Because the dialogue was at the right level, the learner was able to take quite a lot of it on board and make it his own: part of his own internal monologue that he refers to when he thinks about how to do this activity. In other words, there was quite a lot of shared meaning between the teacher and the learner, which meant that the learner could understand a new concept and, therefore, learn. In Vygotskian theory, this is development proceeding from the intermental to the intramental,[2] from dialogue to internal monologue.

---

2 Neil Mercer, *The Guided Construction of Knowledge: Talk Amongst Teachers and Learners* (Bristol: Multilingual Matters, 1993).

To have a teacher who seems to know where the limits of your understanding lie, accepts you for who you are, and is able to understand the way in which you can be successfully led to new understandings is a powerful thing to experience. It gives a feeling of connection and intimacy. It's an amazing feeling to have someone who understands you and can get inside your head with just the right thing to say. As adults we may avoid situations like that because we may not like to feel that vulnerable, but many of us will remember having teachers at school who did that for us.

The shared meaning is the vehicle for new understanding. In my own career, I started off by making assumptions about my pupils, which meant that I made mistakes at step one of this process: I failed to make an accurate assessment of what my pupils did and did not understand. I thought that they would know, for example, what a map of the world looks like. I thought that they would be able to read basic words. I thought that if I told them three instructions, they would be able to follow all of them. Then I revised my assessment to two instructions, and then one, and then I realised that it was not the instructions that were the problem, but my expectation that they could listen. And there were many other ways in which I mistook the actual levels of my pupils' understanding.

However, even when I was starting to get the academic level of my lessons right, I still struggled to make shared meanings.

So here I am, delivering the lesson as described in the previous example. It is a lesson I have planned down to the last detail. 'The pupils can understand this, and they will love it!' I think.

But the first pupil's thoughts are somewhere else. Perhaps it is very windy, and he cannot concentrate. Perhaps there is a thunderstorm coming. It is still two hours away, but this pupil can hear it anyway (hard to believe, but he has been proved right in the past). Or perhaps – as one of my former colleagues used to say – today, for some reason he is simply 'tuned to the moon'.

The next pupil cannot listen because she has pain in her head. Perhaps her parents have never taken her to the dentist and an aching rotten tooth is all she can think about. Or perhaps she was playing on the computer till the early hours of the morning and now has a headache from fatigue, or from all the sugary foods she has been eating. There are so many potential distractions for each pupil.

Perhaps they are preoccupied by their inner demons ...

... or by the fight they have just had or are about to have at break.

Perhaps they have missed out on so many early childhood experiences that they cannot function until they go through some necessary developmental experiences, like play or receiving comfort.

Or their bodies are wracked by a need for sensory experiences.

Or their anxiety levels keep triggering their fight-or-flight response.

Perhaps they come from a family in which listening to each other just never happens, or where ignoring what others say is a strategy that usually pays dividends. Or perhaps they have never been listened to or validated by their caregivers, and do not know how to listen to others.

Or perhaps their anxiety levels have led them to obsess about one particular thing, which they can develop great knowledge about, and then believe, pretend or hope that nothing else matters.

Perhaps their relationships with caregivers have been painful in the past, and the only thing they want to know is when and how you are going to betray them.

Maybe they are just hungry.

Unfortunately, I cannot rely on the degree of reciprocity in my interactions that I would like to see. I know many other teachers, in many other settings, are in the same situation. Many pupils, for a wide variety of reasons, come into the classroom unwilling or unable to engage in the rich shared meanings that we would like them to experience so that their learning can move forward at a pace commensurate with their peers whose lives are more stable. As we will see, on occasion, I have had to put considerable amounts of energy into just getting pupils to stay in the classroom or, once physically back in the room, getting them in a frame of mind so that we can start to create shared meanings together.

Many of the hindrances to participating in shared meanings have a substantial emotional component. But there is yet another way in which emotions can hinder learning. As the example at the start of this chapter demonstrated, the teacher will need to review and revise their interventions according to their assessment of the level of the learner's understanding. This fine-tuning is part of usual practice for most teachers (unless, perhaps, they are lecturing). What is more difficult to cope with is when the gap suddenly appears. Perhaps the learner has come up against a concept which they thought they had understood, but actually they have not.

The gap between the pupil's and the teacher's understanding could suddenly appear for a number of other reasons, of course, such as the teacher going too far or too fast in their thinking, or the learner becoming tired. We will look at what happens when the gap appears, and the shared meaning breaks down, in much more detail later on in the book. For now, the point I want to make is that whenever there is a breakdown in the teaching and learning process, there is always an emotional component to consider, because that is one of the functions of the emotions: to take over our reactions when our ability to rationalise cannot cover a situation. The pupil may now have to handle anxiety, irritation, anger or shame. The teacher will also have to work to manage their own emotions as well as those of the pupil. Because teaching and learning has to operate around the limits of the learner's knowledge, there is always a chance that emotions will be brought into play.

Our emotions are there to help us get through times when cognition cannot cope. We can trigger our fight-or-flight response to get ourselves out of danger, for example. Less dramatically perhaps, they help us to protect our self-esteem and to guide ourselves back to a place from which we can understand what has happened. I call this moment when rational thought breaks down the 'what the hell?' moment, though other expletives have been used, depending on the context. Both participants feel the breakdown in mutual understanding, of course.

For some of us, the drive to learn is constantly pushing us to the boundaries of our understanding, to the limits of our ability to rationalise our experience. We may be comfortable with the darkness of ignorance that lies just beyond our understanding; we may crave to explore it and we may feel we have the emotional wherewithal to cope with whatever it throws our way. We are keen to set out in exploration. For others, our emotions are not sufficiently well-managed for such an adventure to be anything other than traumatic. The drive to learn is tempered or even obliterated by the difficult emotions that are provoked, either by the proximity of the darkness or the challenges we may experience in placing our trust in the teacher as our guide into it. The children in this book tend to be scared of the dark. They are either unable or unwilling to take the risk with their emotions that joining minds with the teacher involves. What that looks like in practice can vary greatly, so I will now tell the stories of two pupils who demonstrate the reluctance, or inability, to make shared meanings in very different ways and, in doing so, expand on key points about the emotional dimension of shared meanings and of learning.

Two case studies – Dean and Phil

The gap in the learner's understanding may come at any point in the learning process. It may be when trying to engage with complexity in the cognitive aspects. For example, the learner may understand most of the process of long division, but not be able to recall where the remainder number goes. Or they can recite pi to five decimal places when they need to remember it to seven. Equally, the gap may be an emotional one. I am an amateur painter, and there comes a time during many of the paintings that I do when I have a crisis of confidence. It's usually a few hours in. I suddenly look at the work with a fresh eye and realise that it is rubbish. Sometimes I go further and think that not only is this present work rubbish, but that it confirms what I have always thought, which is that I actually cannot paint. Sometimes I abandon the work. Then a few weeks later I find it stuffed into a bag somewhere and realise that it's actually pretty good. I should have kept going. I just needed someone to help me bridge the gap in my emotional state, by saying something like, 'Just ignore those negative thoughts. You always get them. Work through them. When you do, you are usually successful. Maybe take a five-minute break to recharge your batteries.'

Dean needed someone to bridge his gaps for him right at the start of the learning process. Before we could even think about getting down to schoolwork, we needed to put a lot of effort into getting him emotionally ready to apply himself. Here was a boy who was not used to the idea of sharing meanings with anyone he did not trust, and that meant anyone in authority in particular.

Dean is 15 and walks everywhere with the swagger of the streetwise boy. It appears to be the walk of exaggerated self-belief, although it does not take much time to realise that, actually, Dean has very little self-belief at all. He thinks that being at a special educational unit is embarrassing because his mates all tell him so, but when he can allow himself to relax away from their glare, he enjoys being with us. Anyway, he knows that his friends aren't attending the mainstream school they should be at, and that they are kind of *losers* (his word), but that does not stop him wanting to be with them and to impress them. His three elder brothers have all been in jail. Dean often says, supposedly jokingly, that he will follow them there. Dean's reading and writing levels are far below where he feels they should be, and he tries desperately to cover this up. But he will spend time with us, learn to trust us and allow us to see just how limited these skills are, so we can work with him at his real ability level, and he will make progress for the first time in a long while. It will turn out that he can achieve far more than he ever thought possible, and he will soon be reading a range of texts independently.

However, having only been with us for a month or so, he is still ready to blow up any time he feels under pressure. Being able to communicate with us is something he is not at all good at. He needs a lot of help with it. And on the day in question he walks in with an almost comically furrowed brow and a petulant protruding bottom lip. We have been expecting this because Dean's mum phoned while he was on his way to school to say that they'd had a row the night before which continued over into this morning. She had caught him with his hand in her purse, so he was sent to his room. This morning he was told that he was grounded, so he told her to fuck off and then walked out without breakfast. Now we are about to ask him to have a go at reading and writing activities that, for the moment, will just underline the sense of failure that is conjoined with the concept of school in Dean's head. So it is not surprising that when another boy sits in the chair that Dean is heading for, Dean pushes the petulance button once more and tells the boy to get the fuck out of his way. Dean is not interested in my insistence upon a peaceful resolution to the situation. Neither is Dean placated when, as he moves towards the boy in an attempt to intimidate him, I step calmly between him and his intended target. He turns, kicks a chair over and storms out, telling the member of staff who goes after him to fuck off and stop following him.

He walks out of the main door and through the car park towards the school gates. This would not be the first time he has walked off, and I know that if it is to become a habit and the school gates become less of a boundary in his head than they are now, we will lose Dean in the doldrums of non-attendance. If we are to achieve some common ground, a shared understanding, it is going to take a bit of work on our part. So when he is not looking I run surreptitiously to get within earshot of him and I say in a voice which hopefully has no sense of threat in it (in order to give him as little as possible to react against) that if he were to leave the premises, we will do nothing to stop him, but we will have to report him to the police as a missing person. With some pupils I might go on to say that the police will come looking for them because they have to when a child with special needs is reported missing, but in this instance that could make things worse. Putting the right boundary in is like tickling a trout: too gentle a touch and the fish will ignore you and swim away, too firm and the fish will panic and take flight.

Of course, Dean's background is such that he cannot let the mention of the police pass without comment, and a few expletives come out as he insists that he is not scared and is going anyway. I do not try to use any of my so-called 'authority' because now he is really looking for something to rebel against. I pay attention to what he is doing, not what he says he is doing. While he is still swearing blind that he is leaving, his pace has slowed considerably. I back off, apologising for the system that makes phoning the police my unavoidable duty. I let him feel angry with the system rather than with me. I turn away from him because he does not want to lose face by being seen not to go through the gates. I sit down on the grass and concentrate on picking the blades, so that I am as unthreatening as possible. After a while the charge of anger has drained from the scene, and I wonder about trying a joke in order to change the mood, but perhaps it's too soon. So I say in a somewhat non-committal, gruff and almost comically manly voice that he's done well to not allow a small problem to become a big one, and now we can go and sort the little one out.

'I'm not going back in there with that cow.'

'Which cow?'

'Mrs Jones. She's always giving me filthy looks.'

'Really? Well, she gives me them too. Come on in, I bet you if you apologise to her, she'll apologise to you.'

To be clear, most of the time I was dealing with Dean I was managing my own anger at what seemed the most tiresomely immature behaviour. When he storms out, I am biting back the desire to judge him or reject him. I am tired, and my first reaction is one of incredulity that such a little misunderstanding has caused such a melodramatic reaction. I am not even sure I believe his anger. This is a toddler tantrum, from someone who is purporting to be big and tough. I am not particularly proud of thinking like this, but it is how I felt at the time. It is natural to feel this way, because that is how interaction works. Troubled children communicate through their behaviour, and what Dean is communicating is precisely the anger that his actions have engendered in me. It is important for me not to try to quash his feelings – or to deny them – but to acknowledge them, and then manage them, contain them, and do something constructive about them. In other words, if we are going to have any chance of creating a shared meaning between us, it is important that I play a significant part in its creation. Left up to Dean, his narratives are self-defeating and lead to his isolation. I need to be able to turn this situation around. I need to understand that he does not yet have the skills to cope with setbacks or with feelings of vulnerability. He has not got a clue about how to resolve conflicts, or even how to connect in any meaningful way with another human being. Dean and I cannot engage if he has walked off into the blue yonder, to his *loser* friend's house down the street.

I did whatever I could to contain him, to stop him from walking off, to manage his emotions for him and get him back into the building, and to negotiate between him and his work and the people he had got into conflict with. I was never going to call the police, but back then I sometimes used a bit of brinkmanship to get what I wanted. It is often said that when managing behaviour, you should never threaten an action that you do not intend to carry out, but I don't really buy into that. I do whatever it takes to put the lid on a certain behaviour, and if that means threatening to phone parents or, in this case, the police, so be it – even if I am hoping that my bluff won't be called. Sometimes it is, and I have had to find creative ways out of carrying out the threat without the undesired outcome. Deliberately misdialling is a useful option. You can threaten to ring again in a few minutes and use the time to work on the situation, bring the child around and obviate the need to do so. Sometimes children seem to need to take the situation to the brink of disaster before they can step back from the edge.

Having got Dean back into the building, we can work on the skills he needs to develop if we are to avoid scenarios like this happening again. But he is so unused to evaluating his own actions, seeing two sides to a story, or even recognising his own emotions and the actions associated with them that only very small steps are possible. While I would love to be able to set Dean back on the right road quickly, his head is still full of anger and now shame. He is still talking about the dickhead pupil who stole his chair, the bitch teaching assistant who gave him a dirty look when he kicked the chair and his stupid mum who gave him hassle this morning and whose fault it is that he has had neither his breakfast nor his first-of-the-day cigarette. So we sit in the office until he is ready to go back into class.

The truth of it is that he is a nicotine-starved addict, with low blood sugar and very few aspirations for self-betterment, whose capacity for negotiating his way through situations in which even the most mild demands are placed upon him needs to be improved if he is going to thrive in life. Over the coming months we can start to chip away at these barriers and build in him some capacity for growth, through the gradual increase in our capacity to make shared meanings together.

With Dean, most of his emotions seemed on the surface and immediate. I have given just a snapshot of the work that we did with him, a description of one event that occurred during the time that he was with us. The same principles relating to the creation of shared meanings apply to the longer conversations between pupil and teacher. Our relationships are not defined simply by the dynamics of the moment. They contain elements which develop over time, such as trust, attitudes and beliefs, which play a part in the nature of the shared meanings that are possible. The next example looks at the difficulties we had establishing an effective teacher–learner relationship over a five-year period with Phil, a boy who was 11 when he first walked through our doors.

Phil came to our school with the label *moderate learning difficulties*. His paperwork did not mention EBD, so he did not initially attend the more specialised section of the school, but went into a class for children with general learning difficulties. His social worker mentioned the behavioural problems that he had demonstrated in previous schools, but she was *sure* (i.e. hopeful) that these had been blips, due to the demands that a mainstream curriculum had placed on him; she *knew* that once he was at a special school, he would be able to relax and start to thrive.

Phil never relaxed. Every time I came across him I knew that something was wrong. After a few years I had developed a radar for the troubled child, something which told me that minor misdemeanours are not just the result of messing about a bit, but part of a bigger and more significant picture of disturbance. My radar would be bleeping away as I saw Phil out on the playing field every break and lunchtime. I could see that the group of boys who flocked around him soon discovered that it was a strain to be with him. Phil wanted to play games that involved quite a lot of rough and tumble, and he resented any exhortation from staff to play gentler games. I once tried suggesting to him that his friends did not like the games he wanted to play, but he looked at me like I was an idiot. He had no idea that he was driving the agenda and that the games were not to his friends' liking. He proved this by asking them in front of me, and gave me an 'I told you so' look when they confirmed that they were fine.

However, a while later his best friend stopped attending school, and the boy's parents cited the stress caused by Phil as a reason. Also stressed by Phil was his class teacher, whose finely tuned behaviour management skills often had no effect on Phil's negligible work rate or on his verbal and physical aggression in class. So, aged 12, Phil was moved to the specialist EBD unit.

He moved on from the unit aged 16, and I am not sure that he learned anything at all in a formal academic sense in the vast majority of the lessons we made him attend. He had some well-crafted strategies for not doing any work at all. He was a very personable lad who could charm one or two of the more pliable teaching assistants into doing his work for him. To be fair, working with him was a very draining experience, and it could seem illogical not to take the easy way out. You could either do the work for him or cause him and yourself 10–20 minutes of grief, at the end of which, if he did the work at all, it would be without any meaningful engagement. It took him at least 10 minutes to settle down to work. Every day he would react to the indication that it was time to start work by going over to his desk, placing one hand on it and one on the neighbouring desk and swinging like a gymnast on the parallel bars. I could see that he was thinking that one day he would swing right over, a full 360 degrees, but he never did it. We would urge him to sit and start his work. He would groan and comply, but then be straight back up again to get a drink, sharpen his pencil, go to the toilet or find the right book. Then he would get distracted by someone else messing about. It was a carefully honed routine, and it lasted for years.

We battled against this reluctance. We set him goals and promised rewards he liked, but his heart was never in the work. We tried to make it as interesting to him as possible. He had a very competitive side, so we appealed to that. While there were small advances in his addition skills or his reading age, they were only temporary. He never engaged with a subject for its own sake, or with learning for learning's sake, and there were many things that he decided were not for him. In the four years he was with us he never had a go at subtraction, because, in his words, 'I don't do takeaways.'

So there were many battles, and it was Phil's mission in life to never lose a battle. However, despite this trait and the many furrowed brows it caused on him and us, his relationships with all the staff were excellent, and he enjoyed being with us. The battles were intense but soon forgotten. In fact, they were only really battles for us, in the sense that he knew he was not going to work, whereas we only thought there was a possibility that he might.

We also had difficulties with his aggression. As with his approach to subtraction, he had a rule in his head with aggression that allowed no flexibility at all. He always got the person back. So, if someone hit him, he hit them harder. Even when play fighting, he always had to have the last and hardest punch, push or kick. This was very tiring, because it meant that no arguments or fights ever failed to materialise because of Phil. He never backed down, and would take anyone on, even when he was one of the youngest pupils in the unit. People learned to avoid provoking him. The staff, however, could not keep out of his way, and he was very aggressive to them too, albeit often in a 'friendly' way. Whenever he came up to talk to one of us, there was always a friendly nudge, push or bump by way of a conversation opener. We could not shake him of this habit. He thought we were making a fuss about nothing again, so we kept a tally of every act of aggression – no matter how small or well intentioned – for a week. There were over 50 each day, but Phil just laughed at us for being sad losers for counting such a thing.

Phil's competitiveness was allied with superb athleticism and coordination. He excelled at every sport he tried. He was a true sportsman too; his need to win everything was tempered by a gracious acceptance of losing to a better competitor (despite being unable to accept losing in any other part of his life). Team sports were not his thing, however, as they required social skills in order to negotiate with teammates and Phil was not interested in that. He loved dodgeball, and for the first year or so that he was with us we went for a session in the gym most days. It was a valued reward for good behaviour and it allowed him to let off steam. He also loved parkour, or free running, and he was very good at it.

Every morning, as he started the daily battle not to do any work, he asked, 'When's lunch?' He could not tell the time and resisted our efforts to teach him. 'I don't want to know how to tell the time. I just want to know when lunch is.' And when he said 'lunch', he actually meant the mid-morning break, which is when he ate his packed lunch. This meant he had to sit through lunchtimes without any food, watching the others eat. He hated this but would not change his habits, such as by bringing in or accepting extra food.

He was fixed in everything he did. I once came up with a way of teaching the times tables that appealed to him. We had twelve cards, each with a multiplication sum in a particular times table written on it (so, for example, 1 x 3 = ?, 2 x 3 = ?, and so on), and a timer pad that you hit to start and finish. The aim was to answer all the cards correctly, in random order, and stop the clock as fast as you could. Phil really liked this, but if he were to answer one question wrong in the first attempt (he often said 3 x 3 = 6, for example, confusing multiplication and addition), then he would invariably make the same mistake every time the card came up from then on. It was the same with language: mistakes stuck. He loved birds, and on a sailing trip around the Isle of Wight he asked me what a particular bird was. I told him it was a gannet. The next time he saw one he said, 'Oh look, there's a janet.' And that was it for the rest of the trip. He could not stop himself making the same mistake each time he saw a gannet, even though he knew it was wrong as soon as he had said it and wanted to get it right. It seemed as though the plasticity of the child's brain, that flexibility and openness to new things that all children should have, and which makes them such great learners, was not there in Phil's case.

Perhaps due to his athleticism and his refusal to back down from confrontation, he had quite a lot of status and was popular among his peers. He was a natural top dog. He was never lonely. In fact, he was the opposite: self-sufficient to the point of frustrating anyone who wanted to be his friend. Melanie, a particularly sensible and kind girl, did her best over a couple of years to befriend him. He had a pet name for her, Lemony, which she liked (though I sometimes wondered if this was another of his mistakes that he couldn't actually rectify), and they spent a lot of time together. The problem was that as soon as there was any degree of disagreement between them, Phil's rejection of her was total. He had no capacity or seeming desire for negotiation or compromise. Melanie initially spent a lot of time trying to repair their relationship whenever this happened, but eventually she stopped chasing Phil's friendship, deciding that it simply was not there in enough quantity or quality to make it worthwhile.

Why was Phil so stuck in his ways, and so closed off to learning? His mother was an alcoholic, to be found most days hanging around on the steps of a local town hall, nearby but far removed from Phil. His dad had tried to look after him and his newborn sister when their mum drifted away, but he chose to do this by taking in a new partner, who had two sons of her own. They were several years older than Phil, who was a toddler at the time. They were very aggressive, so much so that Phil's dad was frightened of them. So, one day he just upped and left, leaving Phil to defend himself and his little sister. Phil did this by developing extreme aggression. He was so small that this must have been only partially effective at best. There were tales of him being thrown out of windows at home. If he put his hands flat on the table, you could see that both his little fingers were shaped like crooked bows, the result of breaks inflicted by his stepbrothers when they teased or tried to control him.

Living in such a situation had made Phil hyper-vigilant, and fearful of any change at all. So even many years later, long after he had been removed from that environment and put into a loving foster home, Phil did not see our attempts to teach him as we did: as efforts to make him into a better version of himself. He just saw it as an attempt to make him a different version of himself, and he rejected this more often than not. Phil's fear of change outweighed any of the arguments that we put to him about the need to grow up and learn, despite the tension that such arguments must have caused within him.

Phil's lack of understanding sometimes caused huge problems. One day, when he was 14, he and another boy terrorised a young female teacher. They sensed her inability to stand up for herself, and made increasingly sexually explicit and aggressive comments towards her until she broke down. Similarly, social workers decided to stop his visits to his sister because they were found kissing in an inappropriate way. But Phil rejected any external or internal pressure to change, despite the impact that events such as these had on him and those around him. The consequences of such actions, while evidently very distressing for the victims of his actions, could be terribly destructive for him too.

Such incidents brought condemnation and negative consequences for Phil. But the only way he was going to move on was if he allowed himself to be helped to become a learner – to develop the ability to share meanings with others – not only so he could take part in formal lessons but in order to develop sufficient empathy that such actions became as unacceptable to him as they were to us.

I do feel that we failed to teach Phil through formal schooling. There were other distressing incidents that I won't report here, but there were a lot of enjoyable times, and I hope we did benefit Phil in some ways. His relationships with staff were rich. He developed a love of birds, and I loved showing him his first buzzard, his first marsh harrier and, of course, his first *janet*. He had a successful work experience placement in a bird of prey sanctuary, where barn owls – his favourite birds – were rescued and cared for. He came on several sailing, camping and surfing trips. Over the course of one week in school we dug a hole in the playing field and conducted our very own archaeological dig (managing to find fragments of a clay pipe and a willow pattern plate). Phil was one of only two pupils who saw the project through; for most, filling the hole back in was a task too far.

Phil never shied away from work that he saw a point to. It was little signs like that, and his seemingly inherent sportsmanship, that made us think that the boy had some resources which he could draw upon in the future. He possessed an inner resilience that his two aggressive stepbrothers had not managed to stamp out of him. It seems that the relationships he had with us, rather than the lessons we tried to teach him, did eventually help him to move forward. He did leave the EBD unit and return to the main classes in our special school after a while, although teachers continued to think of him as work-shy. On the day that he left the school, I shook his hand, wished him well and then gently punched him on the arm. He gave me a look, because he knew that I had challenged him in the game we had played so many times before, the *who can have the last say in the argument* game, where the goal is to be the last one to land a playful punch, nudge or even the faintest of touches, and walk away before the other can retort. Phil's eyes lit up for a second with the fire of his competitive streak, but then he just smiled and walked away.

Chapter 2
The teacher

Becoming the teacher

In the schools that I have worked in, as in many others, pupils are urged to make good choices and act in prosocial ways so that the learning environment can be as harmonious and productive as possible. For example, we teach good listening skills, turn-taking, assertive speaking and so on. In this chapter, in which I focus on the teacher's role in the generation of shared meanings, I show that teachers – the managers of this process of generation – have at least as many choices to make as the pupils do.

I have two abiding memories from the scary early days of my career, when chaos often reigned in my classroom. I do not remember all of the challenging behaviour I was witness to – and part cause of – (perhaps my memory is trying to spare my well-being through this erasure) and these specific memories are both related to my own physical actions. The first was simply tidying my desk. I am not a naturally tidy person, and I was usually happy to have piles of stuff lying around, but there were times when it became very important to me that my desk suddenly got organised. This was always when I was fighting for control of my classroom. I eventually learned to recognise that the urge to tidy up all the books and stationery was a sign that I needed to relax, gather myself and then gather the pupils. After some time, I learned how to not let things get so out of control that an untidy desk became an anathema to me.

How I achieved this control is linked to my second memory, which is of cycling home after a day of stress and trauma, probably after being rescued and patched up by my head teacher. ('Go home, have a glass of wine, and chalk it up to experience.') I would be cycling the few miles to my house in a state of near shock, realising that outside of the little bubble of my classroom the world had still been turning, and that I could rejoin it once I had readjusted from the intensity of the strife of my day. I would start off by cursing the little bastards (because at that point, that was how I thought of them) who had trashed my room and my self-esteem. What particularly sticks in my memory now is what stuck in my craw then: the realisation among the pain and blame that if things were going to be any better the next day, there was only one person who could make that difference happen, and that was me. It was the unfairness of it all that got to me; I had not called anyone a *fucking retard*, or ripped up my work, or insulted someone's mother, or tipped over the desk and stropped off with a pathetic look on my face. No, in fact I had gone out of my way to be nice, had rolled with the first few insults and punches, had tried to stay calm for as long as possible and rescue the situation. Why should I have to change?

But change I did, and the next day I made things right, by making the lesson clearer or more interesting, or by addressing the pupils' anxieties or other difficult feelings. The boys left the class calmly and cheerily, saying, 'See you later, Sir,' and I replied, 'Yes, well done, see you later,' but inside I was clenching my fists in victory, and feeling, somewhat pathetically, as though I had won and they had lost, even if the only way to win was by making them win too. And slowly, over the months, the unpredictability of teaching troubled children turned into something approaching predictability.

How did I get to that point? I started to learn a few lessons of my own. Firstly, I realised that my greatest fear, that I was in danger when I entered the classroom, was misplaced. I had dreaded them ganging up on me, but I soon realised that these children were lone operators, and that they had neither the social skills nor the feeling of common cause to decide to band together against me. Then I realised that there was no such thing as being streetwise, at least not in this context. The bigger the swagger, the greater the vulnerability that was being covered up. I also learned that all the children in front of me were lonely, and desperate to make connections despite their seeming inability to do so. This particular realisation did not make me feel good. If they were desperate, they would seek anyone out, as long as the recipient of their attention was not actively pushing them away. This thought made me reconsider my classroom manner and practice; I needed to become someone who they would approach.

I had also started to learn that there was a narrow window, a small opening in time and space, through which connecting with the pupils – both in a social and in a teaching and learning sense – was possible. I learned to accept what I could not change, such as the amount of swearing that went on across the school or the use of homophobic phrases to express disapproval. Counterintuitively, once I had stopped fighting such causes, I found that my relationship with the pupils improved, so much so that they started to change their language out of respect for me. I also learned to accept the situation if they came to me after an argument with the teacher in a previous lesson, if they were agitated and distracted due to problems at home, or if they were simply tired because they had been up playing computer games half the night. I started to focus my attention on changing what was within my power to, such as the academic level of the lesson, for example, and the amount of warmth and acceptance with which I went about my teaching.

What I did not know then was that it takes strength to create a space for the joining together of two minds. This is especially true when one of those minds is anxious, angry, incoherent or liable to find any sense of balance hard to achieve or maintain. These are children who are only just beginning to learn how to control their emotional state. If they are going to be able to do that, they need someone who is in control of their own mind and, in particular, of their own emotions – someone who will not bring problems of their own to the negotiating table.

We might assume that to be an effective teacher of children with EBD, the most important attribute is patience. This is not true. The most important thing a teacher needs is presence. You have to be there – in the classroom – able, ready and willing to connect. You cannot just wait. You have to act, to bring the pupil to you. You must let nothing divert you. Patience implies sitting though the attrition and waiting for the challenging behaviours to stop. Given how quickly things could escalate, I had to be a lot more proactive than that.

I learned not to take the insults personally. Now it seems an obvious response to have. These are people who hardly know me, so why should their insults matter? Why should I heed anything they say? It is true, on the other hand, that when some children – when they did have a meltdown – went from calling me a *lanky bastard* to a *fat lanky bastard*, I listened to the idea that I may need to lose some weight. But in general, the only message an insult carries is the call for help – they want you to manage the situation for them. It's like a baby's cry. It registers distress but does not tell you what the matter is. It also helped that it became very clear, once I could see past my own insecurities, that these insults really were not about me at all. Moreover, in the pupils' minds everyone around them is so high up on a pedestal that they don't think we will really hear their voice or give their abuse any weight at all.

I am sure people gave me advice to this effect at the start of my career, but it can take a while to internalise such lessons. I probably then made the mistake of overcompensating and putting up with too many insults. Becoming a punchbag is as bad as overreacting to insults. Children don't want someone saying, 'It's all right to abuse me, I'll still be there, I don't mind.' This is an easy trap for a new teacher to fall into in their eagerness to be liked. But you are not there to be liked, not as a friend. These children do not need you to be a friend, because that would mean that you both contribute to the relationship in equal measure, which is not what they need. These children need someone who is going to make their life all right for them, someone who is so in control of their emotions that they have the ability to help the children identify and manage theirs too. That is also why shouting is such a bad idea. In my first term in one school a boy called Karl came up to me and said, in a comic attempt at being surreptitious, 'Sir! Sir! You need to shout at them more, Sir. They're taking the piss.' Given that Karl himself had been one of the ringleaders in the disruption that meant my classroom was now a tip (except for my desk), I gave him a look that said *Et tu, Karl?* and asked, 'And would you like me to shout at you too, Karl?'

He took the attitude of one who had been trying to help, but if his efforts were going to be spurned, he would take his kindness elsewhere, and he left the classroom saying, 'Oh no, if you shouted at me I'd kick off big time.'

So you cannot make the classroom about you but neither can you be a weak presence. I once off-loaded in a meeting with the father of Mark, a 12-year-old boy with the face of an angel who regularly (and seemingly without any triggers) stopped whatever he was doing to proclaim, 'Fuck this shit!' He would then leave the room while tipping over other children's desks. I felt that his father should know just how his son was treating teachers – in particular, how he was treating me. As I started my diatribe, the man was gobsmacked. He explained that in his house, he and his wife could not say or do anything without Mark relating it to what Mr Nelmes thought, said or did. He said he had been looking forward to meeting me to find out just how I had managed to put such a spell over his son. I felt rather churlish, and stopped focusing on how the relationship I had with Mark was making me feel.

However, it is also a mistake to overestimate your own importance. It is tempting to try to become a central figure in a child's life, and to think that if you can promise to always be there for them, then you will be the reason they start to trust again – the catalyst for a new beginning, a new dawn. I learned early on that there are just too many children for such saviour behaviour to be fair, sustainable or even realistic. I had to learn that for some children I was probably the hundredth professional to enter their short lives, and so if they did not invest in me as much as I wanted them to, they were to be forgiven.

I also learned that there were other ways to stop being part of the problem. Daniel, a surly (and slightly scary) older pupil who had very little interest in forming a relationship with me, as he was nearing the end of his school career, regularly talked instead of working in my lessons. I tried cajoling, supporting, sitting near him, nagging, all to no avail. Eventually I said to myself, 'Sod it, this boy has to do some bloody work for me.' Pretending to be calm, I told him that he needed to finish the work before the end of the lesson or stay in at the fast-approaching break time. He looked disdainful of the idea that he was going to stay behind for the likes of me. And, of course, when the bell went and his work was not done, he marched out, ignoring my insistence that he come back. I picked up the work and followed him as he headed to the smoking area across the field (where the older pupils were allowed to get their nicotine fix, to stop them absconding – this was the nineties). I stood next to him, feeling awkward because this area was usually a no-go zone for teachers, and I kept asking him to complete the work. He went from incredulity to annoyance to embarrassment to anger and then walked off, saying that he would never do the work, but in fact he walked back to my classroom. He railed and railed but I could tell that he was going to do it, and he eventually did so, cursing as he left afterwards.

That night I lay awake, worried that I had stirred up a hornets' nest of hatred, knowing that I would be teaching Daniel in the morning. He was there early and asked me if I had seen the match last night. Fortunately I had, and we shared our opinions of it. After that he always did his work and we had a good relationship. By putting in boundaries I had become someone he could relate to and trust, which, it turns out, he wanted more than he wanted to get away with doing no work. I had similar experiences with many other pupils, and with some of the staff too.

Once I had started to become someone strong for my pupils to relate to – someone who understood where they were coming from – life became easier in that trust started to replace distrust, and I could influence what happened in my classroom, mainly through warmth and care, humour and positivity. We cleared room for more fun to happen in our lessons.

Becoming good at engendering compliance was, I thought, the top of the mountain: it is not. Becoming good at engendering compliance is a difficult climb, but it merely gives you sight of the next, higher peak. These children want you to be a safe, containing presence, but they have their own lives to sort out. The time they spend in a classroom where they are understood and cared for is very little in the context of their lives as a whole. So, once they find someone whom they can trust to care for them, and who is not going to bring their own problems to the table, they offer up themselves and their problems for you to deal with. The next peak to climb involves figuring out how to teach them, how to give them the skills and understanding to be able to regulate their own behaviour, so that they can cope and thrive independently.

Adrift in a life with few moral, emotional or social reference points, they will hang on to anything that seems strong enough to hold them. Once they have latched on to you, they will start communicating their problems to you, and they will hope that you can stay strong enough to interpret what is in their hearts – what they need in order to stop the pain they feel. Some of the time you can find a way to help them, and some of the time you cannot. Sometimes, it seems, their pain is just too great. You have to be aware of what is being asked of you, and of whether or not you have the resources in you and around you to deal with it. You have to be aware that you are not going to save everyone, and that when you meet someone you cannot save, you should not sacrifice yourself on the altar of their tragedy.

Later I tell the story of Jayden, a very troubled young man with enormous pain in his heart, who had two successive one-to-one teaching assistants working with him. The first one left because she could not live with such sadness; she could not bear that she was unable to do anything about it. The second was Xavier, a lovely guy who went out of his way to be nice to Jayden, but who was reduced to tears one day by Jayden picking up a computer monitor and, with studied indifference, bringing it decisively down onto the corner of a table, after casually threatening to do so for no apparent reason. When Jayden learned of the distress that he had caused Xavier, he frowned. 'The thing is,' he explained to me, 'I need someone who can cope with whatever I throw at them.' And as utterly selfish and unreasonable though that is, it is the truth. He needed containment, and it was a tragedy that no one was able to provide it. I have made myself into someone who can communicate with, contain, hold and teach as many children as I can, but there are still others who remain out of my reach. There is always the question of whether we can do more, but sacrificing all our resources in an attempt to do so is not the answer.

Establishing coherent meanings

One of the hardest challenges I faced was in thinking coherently about the children in front of me. It was hard to settle on a single view. I saw other teachers have the same problem. Perhaps the best example of this happened in an assembly in a small gymnasium. Its four brick walls and shiny floor cushion no sounds and offer little other comfort. The floor is shiny because this is the first assembly back after the summer holiday and the parquet is a deep chestnut from the polish the caretaker has lavished on it during the break. This space has many memories associated with it. It is the scene of sporting battles – triumphs and defeats remembered well into adulthood. My first memory of it comes from when the head teacher at the time, who showed me round the school on a visit, flipped from being a warm and sensitive man – aware of the difficulties the children face – into a shouting, berating alpha male. On that occasion someone had stolen some money. With any misdemeanour the ritual would be the same: the boys would be lined up around the tramlines of the badminton court that was marked on the floor, and the staff would be watching carefully to see which pupil would be the first to faint, beaten out of consciousness by all the standing and shouting. If the staff did not catch the pupil, there may well be the sound of a skull bouncing off the parquet floor.

This is an assembly, not a bollocking, and the boys are allowed to sit. Some of the 120 chairs that are out in rows for the assembly are missing the plastic plugs in the bottom of their metal legs, so some scratching of the glossy floor is inevitable. The boys file in and sit down. The atmosphere is somewhat tense. Visitors to this school would often talk about how intimidatingly *male* the environment is, and it is true that there is always a whiff of threat in the air. But if you have been here a while, you get used to it, and you realise that even the staff and pupils who contribute to the intimidation are themselves cowed by it. This is an EBD school in the 1990s.

This head teacher is a mild-mannered man, an upstanding citizen. He waits for and gets silence, after a few nudges from staff to certain pupils. The head has a copy of a tabloid paper rolled up in his hand. He starts off by welcoming everyone back to the new term, and says he hopes we have all had a good holiday. The chances are that only a few of the boys will have. Most will have been bored and counting down the days to when they can be back in a place where they are valued and listened to, even if it is only by people who are paid to do so.

The head then talks about his own holiday, which was two weeks in a hotel overlooking a Spanish beach. As he dwells on how nice it was, he loses the full concentration of his audience. He talks about the sun, sea and food, and the company. Do we realise, he asks, that he did not hear one raised voice or a single swear word in all that time? You can see he is reliving the peacefulness of it all.

'And then, sadly,' he continues, 'it was time for my wife and I to return home. When I got on the plane, a very nice stewardess offered me a newspaper. It's this one here, as a matter of fact.' He holds up the paper. He opens it out and there is some arcane political headline across the front.

'I read about what's happening with the government, and I read a bit of sport, because that's what I like to do. And then I turned to pages 2 and 3, and what I saw made my blood boil. I'll admit it, I was angry. I don't get angry often. But when I get angry, it is serious. When I saw what had happened, I was so angry that my fingers were digging into the armrests. My wife asked me if I was all right. I could barely answer. What I had read had upset me so much. Two boys – of the age that some of you are now – two mindless thugs, they had taken it upon themselves to get hold of a breeze block and carry it all the way to a bridge across a motorway, where they dropped it onto the windscreen of a defenceless old lady who was driving along beneath them, minding her own business.'

He shook his head, turned slightly away from the audience, not seeing the smirks of some of the children, who were either so callous that they found it funny or who smile whenever they hear something that makes them nervous or uncomfortable.

'What a senseless, horrible thing to do.'

Another pause.

'I cannot say it strongly enough. It's people like you ...' He looked at his audience, took a breath, and said, 'You people have ...' and then he checked himself, knowing that whatever he thought the boys in front of him were capable of, none of them had been on that bridge, or indeed on any bridge with a breeze block in hand. He was deflated by the sudden obvious gap in his own argument. He said lamely, 'It beggars belief,' and threw the newspaper in a somewhat overdramatic way to the floor. He looked at the faces in front of him, all waiting, only half understanding what he had been saying. He knew he had to change gear, and he did so, because only by being as warm, inclusive and positive as possible did we stand a chance of getting through the day without some major incident. He hoped, he said, that everyone would make the best of the term that lay ahead of us. We all filed out, past the head teacher who was stopping trusted allies, picking out confidantes like the Ancient Mariner, trying to find someone who would fully appreciate the story and the emotions it had engendered in him in the space between the end of his holiday and his return to work.

Some of the children in that audience have since committed crimes every bit as distressing as the one that had troubled the head teacher. Day-to-day life in that school was hard because of the cruelty that the children sometimes inflicted on others. It is hard to be around a child who targets the vulnerable, or who is merciless, relentless or incredibly creative in their violence. The problem is, if we condemn, we cannot establish a shared meaning that is going to help the child.

We have to work with the whole child, and that includes understanding how their lack of ability to connect and empathise with others, combined with their lack of understanding about what drives their own actions, may well create victims.

My first ever such challenge was Kane, a 14-year-old boy whose defining characteristic seemed to be nonchalance. He was nonchalant when he tried to trap my fingers between two desks in the first week I was there, and when he intimidated the other children into letting him have yet another go on the pool table ('We don't mind, Sir,' they would be at pains to convince me, fearful of more trouble later). He had a nonchalant sneer on his face when I took the pool cue off him after he had refused to give it to me. I was inexperienced and allowed myself to get drawn into a win or lose situation. When I exerted some force, he gave up the cue but fell to the ground, claiming injury and the right to sue. Then he got up, came over to me and went to pick an imaginary hair from the neck of my jumper. When I moved to stop him from doing so, he flinched as though from an imagined punch and then he smiled.

These incidents were bad enough, but it was the nonchalance with which he regularly ruined my lessons that really got to me. At any point, it seemed, he would climb over his desk – and often several other boys' – and say that he was 'off' and that he was tired of listening to a dickhead. I would find him later in one of the senior manager's offices, pointing out to them that I was not giving him a chance. He talked then, all nonchalance gone, with a sincerity and respect that made it hard for me to think of him as the same person who had trashed my lesson. There was such a sense of rapport between him and the senior manager that I was left in little doubt as to who was the odd one out in this dynamic.

I resolved to do a home visit, because I sensed his mum had some hold over him. He had talked of being grounded, so I felt I was on the right track. Maybe if his mum and I worked together we would get somewhere. Of course, I was not on the right track at all. What I learned was that every aggressor is also a victim too, because there is always a reason why children display challenging behaviour. Sure, Kane was making some poor choices, but the range available to him was so poor to begin with that he did not stand a chance of making the choices that I wanted him to make. There was some room for personal choice, free will, moral backbone, or whatever you want to call it, in his life but not in the way I thought. I was measuring him against people who, when you match up the demands placed on them by life against the resources they have to draw on to cope with those demands, tend to have some resources to spare.

I began to appreciate that there were two ways of viewing these children, which was what made my life so difficult. They were aggressors, but they were also victims, lost souls adrift on the sea of life. Their actions were also ambiguous. It felt like they were being irrationally hurtful – senselessly destructive – but that feeling was only the result of me judging them from a rather insular perspective. If I could extend my imagination to include their feelings and motivations, then a different interpretation became available.

My determination to make Kane repent his sins and learn by facing the consequences of his actions started to dwindle when I drove into his street. It was clearly not a nice place to live. I did not need to check the numbers of the houses to see which was his. The abandoned fridge and washing machine on the tiny front lawn, alongside the bike with grass growing through the rusty chain, gave it away. The front door was forlorn in a way that I didn't have time to identify before it was opened by someone who was too defensive to be polite. The interior of the house was like that of so many of the houses I was to visit over the coming years. Someone had taken up the carpets and removed the lampshades, as if readying the place for redecoration. The act of stripping this back seemed to have been easy enough, but the act of creating something in its place – of making it nice and so showing care to oneself – seemed beyond the realms of possibility. And so the rough floorboards, the echoic stairs, the piles of stuff put down long ago – just until everything got sorted – and the bare walls marked by a childhood of dirty hands had become the new way to be.

Kane's mum looked equally stripped back, and was unable to offer a smile of welcome. Luckily she talked first, displacing my description of her son with one of her own that gave him some respect, and which was (unlike mine) based on Kane's needs. Consequently, it was tragic rather than righteously indignant. She explained that Kane used to have friends but now that they had outgrown him, they all picked on him. He would have liked to go out but it was dangerous for him to do so, because he would get hurt or be used to run errands for people who did not care about him. He'd always been like this. She'd had nothing but negative messages from a succession of different schools. Maybe he had 'that ADHD', but in any case she did not know what to do because she knew that she was losing the ability to keep him safe or even to connect with him. His dad had left when he was three, but that had been a blessing because he had been quite violent, though she thought Kane was too young to have picked up on that. Was there any chance that he might be able to read one day soon, she asked, because underneath it all she thought he might be quite bright.

I left chastened. The next day I welcomed Kane with a new attitude, determined to be a positive element in the miserable existence it seemed he had to endure. However, within ten minutes I was sick to the back teeth of the little shit and never wanted to see him in my classroom again.

Over the following months, however, I closed the gap between these two views of Kane. I bought a book on ADHD, adopted some of its recommended strategies, and then lent it to Kane's mum, who said it made her cry because it was like reading a book about Kane himself. Nowadays, after meeting many pupils like Kane, I have a fairly integrated view of such children. I can see them from both sides at the same time. I have had to adapt my view, because to not do so leads to madness, to burnout. There were several staff who, on some mornings, arrived at the school gates only to find that they could not cross the threshold. They had just had enough of the attrition and could not take one more seemingly gratuitous verbal or physical attack. Some members of staff may have gone into the profession with some element of idealism, I suspected, but had lost it all to a cynicism that was eating away at them and those whose lives they touched. Others tried to see only the good side and were in denial about the darker side.

Kane and I ended up with a positive relationship, due mainly to adjustments in my behaviour. He was, I learned to see, on his own journey of discovery, looking for a way to connect with others. His journey was not going to be an easy or straightforward one. It might end prematurely, with him deciding that he had gone as far as he could, and that learning or self-improvement was no longer an option, but I was not going to be one of the people who had pushed him into that decision.

In order to give Kane a chance, I had to abide by a rule that I would potentially place before all others: you have to like them. No child wants to, or should have to, enter into shared meanings that are tainted by disapproval and condemnation.

There needs to be acceptance, celebration and hope. If you cannot like them, you should become someone who can, or, failing that, find another job.

The concept of naughtiness as a barrier to coherence

Becoming strong enough to fulfil my role in the creation of shared meanings also meant that I needed to change the philosophy that was underpinning my actions. My theoretical understanding had to adjust in order to catch up with the lessons I had been learning in practice. The first few years were marked by chastening moments of clarity, some of which I have already detailed. The most significant thing I needed to learn dawned as more of a gradual realisation, as the numbers of children and their problems stacked up in my experience: there is *always a reason* for their challenging behaviour.

I needed to rethink my assumption that some children are just *naughty*. This term is unhelpful because, by definition, it involves an external judgement. Being naughty really means not accepting someone else's view of what should happen, which is what we mean when we say things like, 'He is not doing what he has been told,' or 'She is disobedient.' I began to believe that there is *no such thing* as naughtiness. This statement takes some explanation.

In many schools, individuals are encouraged to *make the right choices*. I say these very words to pupils too, but it is actually a ridiculous thing to say. Who would weigh up two options, realise that option A is good for them and option B is bad for them, and then – deliberately and despite this – choose option B? Telling people to make 'the right' choice ignores the complexity of what it means to be human, which we all navigate in deciding how to live our lives. We can all struggle with choice. There are so many factors to consider: short- and long-term costs and benefits, the impact on others, ethical issues and our ability to appreciate the consequences, to name just a few. So, for example, faced with the choice of a second doughnut or not, I know the calories will not help me with my desired weight loss, but I may still choose to eat it because my short-term pleasure may take precedence at that particular moment over my longer-term desire to be slimmer.

As another example: I can't claim to have never acted impulsively in anger. I was once in a rush to finish a DIY task when I noticed that the store I had just arrived home from had given me the wrong size screws. I was driving back across town to replace them, already annoyed, and realised I had forgotten my wallet. I returned to the house and left my car in the alley at the back while I went in to look for it. I was searching, and cursing my own ineptitude, when I heard an incessant beeping of a car horn outside. An elderly lady was determinedly banging on her horn, claiming that I was blocking the way to her garage, despite the fact that she could easily get past or take a short detour and go round the other way. She kept banging on the horn even when I went over to talk to her through the open car window. I grabbed her by the arm to take her hand away from the horn: a split-second decision that I know was wrong rationally and morally, but from an emotional point of view it felt right, until I realised what I had done. Kicking my own garden gate as I went back in had the same effect. It helped me to discharge a few feelings, but I would have preferred to kick something I did not later have to repair.

So 'make good choices' actually means lots of things beside make a choice. It means see the bigger picture, keep your goal in mind, possess the requisite level of emotional development, don't be egocentric, don't let other feelings bleed into this situation, think long term, appreciate the consequences of your actions, be empathetic, see other people's needs too, and recognise and manage your own emotions accordingly so that your action will be the right one for others as well as for you. It's a big ask.

When children mess about in school, it could be for a number of reasons that are quickly fixed – such as the rules not being clear – or because the child is finding out where their own or other people's boundaries are. They could be bored by the lesson. They could also be feeling disenfranchised or in deficit. Being a bit of a clown could be giving them respect from, or intimacy with, peers that they cannot gain through their academic achievements or through more prosocial behaviours. Messing about can be great fun.

We have to accept, therefore, that children's paths of self-discovery do not always fit in neatly with our desire to instil order. We have to build some degree of tolerance of this type of behaviour into our teaching and parenting, and this is true with most children.

Most children, however, thankfully do not go to the extremes that are seen in genuinely troubled children, for whom a different level of response is required. There may be the need for greater supervision and support to ensure the safety and well-being of the pupil displaying such behaviours, but essentially the response is the same. We need to accept that even so-called disruptive acts will have seemed the most rational choice at the time. What we need to do as teachers is discover why that was so. We need to make sense of their actions for them, and this is discussed in more detail later on. To dismiss such actions as merely naughty would be to fail to understand them.

Disparity in adults' views

Understanding the reason for challenging behaviour is the starting point for rationalising interventions to change it. Often, this understanding comes most quickly when the adults working closely with a child share their thoughts. It can help to collectively reflect on questions such as:

- What are the circumstances in which the child displays prosocial behaviours?
- What are the circumstances in which the child displays challenging behaviours?
- What are the triggers for the challenging behaviours?
- What are the early warning signs that challenging behaviours are about to start?

Such questions help us to analyse the behaviours and so inform practice. If you know the triggers, for example, then you can avoid or mitigate against them, and so help prevent challenging behaviours from occurring.

Our understanding of the child's emotions and thoughts which accompany or provoke the behaviours can also be explored by asking questions such as:

- What emotions do the challenging behaviours provoke in you, the adult?
- What skills or knowledge does the child need to be taught in order to meet their needs without resorting to challenging behaviour?

The answers to these questions can be complex and multilayered, and it can be difficult to get to the bottom of what lies behind some children's behaviours, as can be seen in the examples in this book. The answers become all the more difficult to discover when the adults hold disparate views about a child's behaviour.

In order to promote shared understandings among the adults involved with a particular child in our school, we use a range of strategies:

- We maintain a positive ethos, underpinned by values such as inclusivity, openness and acceptance that mistakes can be made and moved on from.
- We conduct full investigations of any incident so that the meanings established about it are as close to the truth as possible. If there is doubt, accusations are withdrawn.
- We report challenging behaviour as objectively as possible, without value judgements – such as, 'He was a nightmare today.'
- We ensure that more positive reports go home than negative ones.
- We foster close relationships with parents.

Occasionally, understandings are easy to establish and share. I was once asked to observe an 11-year-old boy who was, according to his form tutor, 'wrecking all the lessons he went into'. I watched him for a morning. Robert arrived for his lessons a bit late and seemed detached from everything around him. He could not follow instructions simply because he was clearly not listening to them, or not hearing them. He wandered aimlessly around the room, seemingly in a little world of his own, even when the teacher was addressing the whole group. It was distracting for everyone, but Robert did not seem to realise the effect that he was having. I had seen far worse behaviour, but this was a mainstream school with a reputation to protect, so I guess he was 'wrecking' the lesson in that regard. I asked him to come to my office with me, and he complied straight away. There was no sense of him worrying about who I might be, or whether or not he was in trouble. He sat across from me with an open face, though his top lip looked sore because he kept sucking it against his lower teeth.

Robert seemed only vaguely surprised and even less interested to learn that the teachers thought his behaviour was a problem. When I asked him to judge his behaviour he shrugged; he had no views on the matter. I was not sure what to do. He seemed calmer than me. He certainly seemed less interested in the outcome of the conversation than I was. I was having to do all the talking and felt that the more I was going to talk, the less he was going to hear and contribute.

I said that, from what I had seen, his behaviour seemed a little unusual, but there may be a reason for that. And although people have said that children who mess about in class are either mad, bad or sad, I had never met anyone who was mad and I did not believe that children were bad, so that just left sad. I could have been talking about yesterday's weather for all the interest Robert seemed to be showing, but I carried on, ignoring my fading hope that this conversation was going to lead to anything. I said that everyone gets sad sometimes. I had been sad last year, because my dog had died, and that had made me behave in ways that I would not normally do. For example, I –

'My dog died,' Robert blithely interrupted.

'Okay,' I said, 'when was that? Was it recently?'

'Yeah, quite recently. It was a week before my Gran died and a week after my Nana died.'

And that was the end of the discussion, as far as Robert was concerned. That was the problem. Robert was not sure how to cope with these events and they had knocked him out of himself. He needed and received help with his grief. There was still more work to be done, because Robert did not recover his connection with life overnight. A week or so later an older boy suggested to him that instead of going to school, they could go shoplifting in a town ten miles away, which they could get to by sneaking a ride on a train. Robert could not see anything wrong with going along with this. So we had to try to contain Robert, closely supervising him to keep him safe until the relationships he had with us at school and with his family at home could slowly pull him back to reality, and he could deal with the pain that reality had recently caused him. But once that had happened, Robert never displayed problem behaviour again.

Disagreement among the adults, however, makes it more difficult to achieve a positive outcome following our interventions. It seems unfair to expect the child to hone their ability to develop shared meanings with the adults in their life if those adults are offering different and sometimes contradictory starting points from which to engage.

What follows are some brief examples of instances in which I've experienced the struggle to establish shared meanings, each for different reasons.

Disparate emotional climates

Dave and Diana were foster parents to Jack, a boy who had experienced domestic violence and no small degree of neglect before being taken – much against his understanding and his wishes – into care. Jack seemed to have settled in well with his new carers and they were struggling to even believe, not to mention understand, some of the actions he had taken at school, which we subsequently described to them. They evidently felt that we were not handling Jack well. Diana came in to spend a day with Jack to see for herself. She seemed curiously out of touch, perhaps taken aback by the way in which Jack was warm to and joked with the staff. She found some of his actions silly, saying that he was not like this at home.

Diana explained her point of view to me. At home, Jack could be so much more mature than he was being at school. She had been horrified to see him gesture loftily to a teaching assistant to indicate that his laces were undone, expecting her to do them up for him. Not only could he tie his own laces, but he would never dare to command someone like that at home. I explained my theory about his two modes of interaction, his oscillation between subservience and attempted dominance, which is perhaps to be expected when his role model when young was someone who ruled via fear and aggression. I also explained that children with difficult feelings often look to explore them in only one context, and often behave well either at home or in school, but not both. Diana did not agree with me. All she saw was that we were letting Jack get away with things. She was also appalled by his use of baby talk. At home his speech was more refined, with longer sentences, subclauses and no missing articles. She said that she would only be happy when he could show the same coping skills in school as he did at home.

I had to admit that she had a good point. But I replied that I would be happy when he could show the same vulnerabilities at home as he did in school. He clearly was not using home to explore any of his darker, more difficult feelings, and sometimes that left little room for manoeuvre. For example, Diana had recently phoned me to say that Jack's scheduled operation on his ear (he needed a cochlear implant) was going to have to be postponed because he was refusing to go. There was no mention of any discussion having taken place. I asked Diana if she would like us to talk to Jack and she was keen. Once his teaching assistant had explained the operation and shown him a visual calendar – which included a countdown to the operation and a representation of how many days of school he would miss (which had been his biggest worry) – and helped him to explore the feelings he had in relation to this event, he agreed to have the operation. Diana was amazed that we could support him like this and give him the confidence to face the operation.

Disparate beliefs about child development

Seth was too young for our provision but was admitted anyway because there was nowhere else suitable. He was very personable; his voice and mannerisms were suggestive of a particularly lovable Disney character. Seth lived in the present only, and so put a lot of energy into forging friendships for the time in which he was with someone. As soon as the conversation was over, the relationship was too. Nothing would be carried over to the next meeting. Seth had a very limited short-term memory. He did not remember what lesson he was in, what day it was or what events had happened or were about to happen. We gave him the simplest password to get onto the computer, but he rarely got as far as attempting to put the password in because he had often forgotten what he was doing by the time the computer had turned on.

He seemed oblivious of so much. He would pick fights with much bigger children because he was unable to understand what would happen if he provoked them. He could not work for a reward because as soon as he started working, he would forget about the incentive. I tested this once by bringing in his favourite chocolate bar and promising him that he could have it as soon as some maths was done. Even with the chocolate there in full view he could not keep it in mind. Most of the time he would try to do work, but gave up the very second it became hard, or when he felt tired or bored. If he was cajoled by staff, he would become aggressive because he could not understand why they were trying to make him do something that he had no intention of doing, forgetting that he had agreed to it just a few moments before.

His longer-term memory was more robust. He could remember facts that he had learned when he was much younger. And he could remember the incident that seemed to have marked the division between remembering and not remembering.

One day he told the whole class the story of how his mum had crashed the car, which he was in too, and died. He had witnessed her death. He could not remember the age he had been, but he was four. Using the intonation of someone who might have been playing storyteller to an audience of infants, he added, 'and I think she crashed because I was play-fighting with her at the time.'

At first I was gobsmacked. How could he be so honest and aware? But then I began to realise that there was something fishy going on. The story itself was factually correct: apart from the play-fighting bit, to which there were no witnesses, it could be substantiated by his grandparents. What was peculiar was how Seth told the story. The words came out of his mouth, but he was not telling it. Not the real Seth, anyway. I started researching post-traumatic stress and dissociated states of mind. I was thinking about the lack of consequence that Seth displayed, and how that was not surprising, because if you started to let this come into your life, you had to face up to the cause and effect that you may have had on your own mother's death.

My view, however, was not really shared by his grandparents. They were under a lot of pressure, and still seemed to be dealing with the effects of the trauma themselves. Their version of what was happening blamed us for Seth's lack of learning. The reason for his lack of progress, they concluded, was that he was too young for the unit, his behaviour had deteriorated because of the poor example set by the older boys (and I had to admit there was some truth in that), and we were too soft. We should use punishments and deterrents more. The best place for Seth, they decided, was a mainstream class, and a strict one at that. Even before he moved, we had another problem to deal with: I had to report to them that over several break times Seth had befriended a boy several years younger than him, and then one day he had – calmly and with a smile on his face – taken this boy behind a shed in the playground and punched him full on in the face for no externally discernible reason. For me it was symptomatic of Seth's disturbance, and a possible harbinger of future violence that could cause great tragedy. His granddad talked about boys being boys. We never did see eye to eye and Seth was placed elsewhere.

Disparate interpretations of behaviour

One of the most disturbing episodes of my career related to Lee, a boy who we worked with for five years, but saw little or no sense of progress in the most worrying aspects of his behaviour. Within the first year that Lee was with us, I tried to report my concerns to the relevant authorities: he seemed too disturbed to be taught by the likes of us. They told us to get on with it, or permanently exclude him if his actions warranted it. Given that we put up with all kinds of challenging behaviours from a range of pupils, and were reluctant to add to the sense of rejection that has featured in so many of their lives, the latter was not going to happen.

However, so much of what Lee did seemed ominous. Every drawing he did featured fangs, guns, knives and blood. Every possible reference to abusive sex was inferred from anyone's speech, however innocuous, and celebrated. The staff started to be circumspect about using the word 'it', because if a double entendre could be inferred, Lee would infer it. Moreover, he relentlessly followed his own agenda, working only when he wanted to. He seemed to be locked in his own dark world. Occasionally the consultant paediatrician would phone me up and ask me for an update on Lee. Grateful for the chance to speak to someone who could understand – and finally able to process my concerns – I tried as objectively as I could to describe Lee's proclivities and fantasies, and how on several occasions he had become so violent that we had actually called the police. The consultant would listen politely and then thank me for the information, but then say that all he really wanted was an update of Lee's height and weight, to check that his ADHD medication was at the right dosage.

Lee's mum was a feisty woman who told it as she saw it. She would ring me some mornings at around 8.30, to say that Lee had just been picked up by transport, and if he came in telling me that she had trapped his fingers in a drawer on purpose, then he would be absolutely correct because she had told him to stay out of the drawer many times. She thought nothing of telling the professionals who met many times to discuss Lee's progress, or the lack of it, just what she thought. She thought the defining characteristic of all Lee's behaviour was the sexual dimension. The *bloody social workers* could come around as often as they liked and talk about letting Lee have some responsibility as he got older, but she was not going to let him out into the community because he was not safe. She could not leave him alone with his younger sisters because he was cruel to them. Occasionally she got sick of us all and stormed out, leaving the social worker to opine that therein lay the problem: his behaviour was not especially sexualised; it was challenging because of poor parenting, and because – it was suspected – Lee had been the product of rape, which explained why his mum had never bonded with him. The sexualised element came from her invention, not from his behaviour. Shortly after leaving us, however, it was alleged that Lee had been sexually abusive to his younger sisters over a number of years.

Disparate philosophies

An interesting feature in this battle for meaning that we can get into when interpreting children's behaviours and their lives is that it includes considerations of free will and determinism, although it is rarely phrased as such. We all have opinions on the concept of free will, and sometimes the language around this can become laden with judgement – for example, through the use of terms such as moral fibre, backbone, etc. This can inform whether we decide that a child is worthy of extra support or whether they should just *buck their bloody ideas up* and fit in. These beliefs can underpin the attitudes of professionals, even if they rarely express them.

Frank was a 15-year-old boy with autism who had barely attended school when he came to our unit. Our carefully prepared induction programme, designed to help him overcome his anxieties, was regularly trashed by his absolute refusal to do anything more than come into my office for a cup of tea. He often refused to even leave his house to get in his mum's car, or if he did get in the car, he refused to get out when he got to school. These refusals were delivered with a cheeky grin, and often a little joke that was funny only to him. Various professionals talked (away from the official meetings) of his lack of *oomph*, or lack of *moral fibre*, and of his *taking the piss*. This had all been implied if not overtly suggested to his mum over the years, and she was tired of it all. In fact, on a couple of occasions she had driven off into the night, only to come back days or weeks later, so beaten down was she by the pressure of these interpretations. She felt accused of complicity in Frank's non-attendance, although of course this was never said in the official meetings.

Eventually Frank's refusals to attend built to a head, and his placement was up for discussion – as was the possibility that his parents may face prosecution for his non-attendance. We all had our opinions of course, but in official terms these counted for nothing. The only person deemed to have the authority to pronounce on the matter was Frank's paediatrician, and the day had come for him to conclude whether this non-compliance was something Frank could not help, or whether it was something more egregious – a lack of willingness to grow a bit of backbone, an act of moral cowardice by him with his mum as accomplice.

The paediatrician was late to the meeting, so we chatted about Frank's predicament. County education officers who had never met Frank or his mum before asked if she had tried using reward systems – such as stickers or tick charts on the fridge. Frank's mum – a veteran of many professional attempts to manage Frank's behaviour – wilted at such questioning, as she had tried every technique several times over. Her anguish was only heightened when the paediatrician came in and was asked by the chair of the meeting to pronounce on whether Frank was unable or just unwilling. The paediatrician took his time and then said that maybe we were asking the wrong question. We all pondered this new turn – it had the ring of something philosophical which was going to take our thinking onto a new level. Or possibly not, because then the paediatrician wondered aloud if Frank's reticence to come to school was down to him not liking cars. *Maybe he gets travel sickness?* Everyone in the room groaned inwardly. Frank's mum never did get prosecuted but neither did Frank attend our or any other school, which was okay, he reassured me on the occasion of my last attempt to get him to come, because he intended to travel to the United States, become a wrestler and make lots of money.

Towards a coherent philosophy of childhood and its implications for the educator

The children I have worked with most successfully are those children who I have been able to understand. Without such an understanding of who they are and the pressures they face, it becomes very difficult to create shared meanings with them and so build their capacity to learn. No matter how I might feel about the nature of some of their actions, I believe they need to have someone who can understand where they are – and meet them at least halfway – if they are going to be able to overcome the obstacles that are preventing them from making progress in their learning.

However, as the examples I've related in this chapter show, this can be problematic. Accepting that you have to like them and that there is always a reason for their challenging behaviour brings another question to the fore: is to understand always to forgive?

I do not believe I have ever taught a child who is evil at heart, or who was somehow predestined to be mostly damaging to those around them. Even with Lee, who I described previously, it was clear that he was driven by extraordinary levels of anxiety. His story shows that there are some children who are difficult to connect with; it is a challenge to cut through their damaging behaviours to the child behind. As some of these children have got older, their vulnerable side – the lost and lonely soul behind the anger, anxiety and aggression – has become harder to find and connect with. A handful of this group have gone on to the point where their actions, perhaps through habit, perhaps through some kind of psychological vicious circle, have become so consistently damaging to those around them that talk of their good side – their lost and lonely side – has become academic. Indeed, given the hurt they cause, it can seem churlish to raise the issue.

Interacting with troubled children, therefore, raises some very basic questions about the nature of children and of what it is to be human. How we perceive children is a philosophical touchstone. Are they blank slates, waiting for their experiences to write their character for them? Are they angels or devils in disguise? Are we all inherently selfish until we realise that we have our own needs met through a semblance of giving and taking?

I do not profess to have the answer, but it is important to ponder such questions because they will inform how you treat these children. My take on it is this: having taught hundreds of damaging children, and seen that they are equally as damaged, and having just about managed to like them all, my view of the human heart is quite a positive one. While capable of great cruelty, it does by nature bend towards kindness. And children in particular? Actually, I tend towards the view of the Swiss psychologist Alice Miller, who sees children as being naturally more in touch with their core emotional state than we adults, whom she criticises for often (consciously or unconsciously) acting upon children in ways that seek to render them as disconnected from their emotional centres as the adults are themselves, because being around someone who is in touch with themselves is a threat to those of us who are not.[1] The implication of this view chimes with a central message of this chapter, that we need to look at ourselves at least as much as at the children when considering the drivers behind their actions.

---

1   Alice Miller, *For Your Own Good: The Roots of Violence in Child-rearing* (London: Virago Press, 1983).

Chapter 3
The context

Acknowledging the power of the context

A couple of years into my career, as I was starting to get the hang of effective classroom management, I overheard two boys discussing their experience of the school. One was new and was being given advice by the other. The new boy wanted to know which teachers were strict, and which were not. I was still struggling with trying not to shout or use my size or physical presence to intimidate in a school where other teachers were doing just that. I, along with several other teachers, wanted the children to be able to regulate their own behaviour, rather than to simply be obedient. My confidence in my ability to achieve this was still quite low, so I was surprised when the advice-giver named me as one of the strictest teachers in the school. Later, I asked some other pupils for their views, and they surprised me too. In their view I was the strictest. They explained that while they knew they were not going to get shouted at or punished, they also knew that they were not going to get away with anything. If they messed about, they knew it would be followed up, not by anger but by an insistence that they reflect on it, think about what their aims were and about how they could have achieved them more effectively without the destructive aggression that was so often the first (if not only) choice in their toolbox. Boundaries would be agreed and put in place, and expectations for good behaviour in the future would be raised.

At the time I was surprised because I felt that I'd had to give up so many of my preconceived notions about good behaviour. I had accepted a certain degree of swearing, as I mentioned. But I reflected that the tide had turned, and I was now able to claim increasing influence over the meanings created in my classroom. What I had done, in fact, was learn to accept that, as the teacher, I did not have sole control over these meanings. While I had become more able to influence events in the classroom, I realised too that the learner and the context play a part. This chapter explores the role of the latter in more detail.

All communications depend in part on context for generating meanings. The same utterance can vary wildly in meaning depending on where and when it is said, and on what happens immediately before and after. As already mentioned, it would have been nice to be able to assume, as perhaps some teachers can and do, that when you plan a lesson, you can be sure of the meanings that will be generated. With troubled children this is just not possible; you can plan your lesson and, indeed, any encounter you like, but your success in making a connection will depend not just on how you act out your plan, but on how you react to the other person's reactions to your actions. You have to be present right there, right then. Teachers have to teach like singers have to sing; even if you have sung the same song or taught the same lesson many times over, you have to mean it each time, or your partner in the interaction – the audience or the pupil – will know that you are faking it, that your heart is not in it, so they will hold back too.

In fact, in the early days, I started to notice that the greater the detail in which I planned a lesson, the greater the chance that it would fail. I believe this happened because the more I planned, the more I tried to wrestle too much control over the meaning of the lesson for myself. Later I became more adept at incorporating flexibility into my planning to allow for the voice of the pupil and the role of context.

I learned to accept that meanings are never repeated. You can teach the same lesson in the same classroom, but the context has changed because the time of day or year is different, and, of course, the learners are different. It is a different lesson, even if all the factors that are within your control are the same. That's why it's hard to teach teaching; there is no foolproof formula for making meanings. You don't always have control of all the components, because you can never be sure what variables and, especially, what emotions are going to be in the room at the time.

There are so many contextual factors that affect the meanings made in the classroom. The colour of the walls, the size and layout of the room, even the type of flooring (and the way it affects the acoustics of the room) can all play a role. For my pupils, I had to ensure that the flightier ones were not given desks close to the doors or windows. I had to ensure that pupils who sparked off each other were kept sufficiently far apart. I had to be aware if there had been arguments or fights at break or lunchtime. There were so many factors, and it was never possible to identify all of them. I even learned to think about the weather's influence; there seemed to be a strong correlation between windy days and an increase in challenging behaviours, for example. Other colleagues swore that the full moon brought out the worst behaviours, but I never explored this possibility.

In this chapter, I consider just three of the most common and most influential factors that I encountered and had to deal with. These factors encircle and frame the shared meanings of the classroom like rings on an archery target. Working outwards from the bullseye, we have the immediate environment of the classroom and the school. Then we have the wider present, which is the pupil's home experiences. The widest ring of them all, by far, is the pupil's past.

The classroom and school environment

There have been significant changes in child safeguarding and in our understanding of the causes of challenging behaviour over the three decades of my career. Some of the contexts I worked in now seem impossibly unregulated and wild in comparison to current standards. I remember two pupils entering my classroom for a lesson, keen to tell me a joke. It started, 'There were two cunts walking down the road …' I stopped them and said that they could not use language like that. They assured me that it was fine to do so, as they had heard the joke from Mr X, the teacher of their last lesson. Back then, I wanted to be able to put in boundaries, in part for my own well-being. I didn't want to hear swearing, and prohibiting jokes like this one was done partly with my interests in mind. I did not realise what is obvious to me now, that boundaries are primarily there to keep children safe and secure. They need and want to know that the social and moral structure of the school is safe and healthy, and although teachers telling jokes like this could cause short-term excitement and jest, in the long term it was detrimental to pupils feeling safe, and therefore detrimental to the ethos of the school.

It was not for prudish reasons that I worried about the quality of the school ethos as a context for teaching and learning. There can be a feeling of precariousness in schools for troubled children: that you are struggling to stay ahead of the game, or to cope with all that is thrown at you. There is also a feeling that if things start to go downhill, the speed with which they do so can accelerate quickly. The pupils who tried to tell me that joke were in a school in which things were starting to go downhill fast. The head teacher was asked to work more closely with the local authority, which had, in the past, turned a blind eye to certain practices (such as the smoking area) but now wanted greater accountability. The head subsequently left and staff absence increased, as did the incidence of serious behaviour challenges. Staff and pupil anxiety started to rise, there were more incidents that were so serious they involved children having to be restrained, and within a few years the school was closed. I had left the school before its closure, vowing that I would get out of any similarly deteriorating situation in the future much more quickly, such was its effect on my mental health and sense of professional competence and confidence. Later I explain how to ensure that the ethos of the school provides the best possible context to allow troubled children to thrive.

Home experiences

Early in my career I realised the importance of understanding each pupil's home circumstances and of meeting their parents or carers. I'll illustrate this with another example of one such home visit.

Maizzie's house stood out from its neighbours because of the evident lack of care of the frontage and garden. I walked into a tiny hall which, along with the stairs, was stripped of carpets and wallpaper. Sadly, it was easy to tell that this was not due to an ongoing process of decoration. Scratching manically behind a door was the family dog. Despite her mother's instructions, Maizzie let the dog into the hall. It was absolutely thrilled to be allowed to greet the stranger in the midst. It was impervious to all entreaties or commands to leave me alone and go back into the kitchen. Eventually, I felt I had to lend a hand in proceedings as we were getting nowhere. I went to the kitchen door, hoping the dog would follow me. As it did, I encouraged it to carry on its journey back into the kitchen with what I hoped were kind words and a gentle hand. It was a successful manoeuvre, or so I thought. Maizzie's mum did not agree. Though well over a foot shorter than me, she faced up to me and told me that 'No cunt pushes my dog. If I want a cunt to push my dog, I'll find my own fucking cunt.' Then, without missing a beat, she politely invited me through to the living room.

The living room had the sweet smell of a place that had not been cleaned in a long time. I can be slobbish myself, but I felt it best not to sit too far back into the sofa. The floorboards were specked with islands of once-black carpet adhesive that gathered dust and detritus. It seemed as though Maizzie's mother found thinking things through quite difficult, and in the conversation that followed she relied on Maizzie, who ungraciously explained anything that I had worded in too complicated a way. All the while, Maizzie directed angry looks at her mum and tight little smiles at me.

There were clear signs of aggression or anger in their relationship, and neglect of the physical environment of the home; however, these were not Maizzie's main problems. When Maizzie joined us, we were contacted by a social worker who told us that there had been some investigations, but these had been resolved and now social services were closing down their involvement with the family. I asked for the paperwork relating to the social services' involvement but was told that there was no need for us to have this. The only detail I was given was that the partner of Maizzie's mother, John, was not allowed to reside in the house. I was told that he had subsequently moved out. And yet, here he was, sitting in an armchair, a few feet away.

I had some serious concerns about this man long before I had met him, and reported all of them to social services. I had subsequently found out that the paperwork I had been denied contained details of Maizzie's older sister's allegations that he had abused her, and that her mum had shouted from downstairs to tell her to be quiet while it was happening. The sister had retracted the allegation. We reported any signs of possible sexual abuse that related to Maizzie, and the inappropriate sexual talk that other pupils said Maizzie engaged in. We reported that when we took the pupils on a residential trip for a week, Maizzie rang home every night in front of us all to speak to John, rather than to her mum. For five nights he did not come to the phone, and Maizzie talked to her mum with a mouth full of chewing gum and a scowl in her voice. When she put the phone down, she explained that John could not speak to her because he was busy watching a soap opera on TV. On the last night he did design to speak to her and the change in her voice was chilling. She went from a stroppy, couldn't-give-a-damn teenager to a trying-hard-to-please, cute little 8-year-old in the time it took her mum to hand him the phone. Her mood was very positive for the rest of the evening. Mine not so much.

So during that visit I felt that having John in the room with us may be of interest, because it may help me to help social services to protect Maizzie. I thought he would leave, but he did not. He merely avoided all contact with me by reaching behind him for a small cushion and placing this over his face. It was soft enough to mould to his nose and hang there without needing to be held. He sat faceless like that for the quarter of an hour or so it took me to explain to Maizzie's mum why I'd had to bring Maizzie home in the middle of the school day.

This home visit was typical in some ways. It was typical because it helped me to understand where Maizzie came from. It helped me to understand that her need to feel safe and validated was not being met, and why that appeared in the classroom as sudden mood swings, when she would switch from being a tightly smiling people-pleaser to a destructor who is plunged into the darkest mood and just wants to put a bomb under everything. Sadly, it was also typical from a socioeconomic point of view. I often visited houses where parents were struggling financially, and this had a number of ramifications for the family's well-being.

Additionally, we often found it hard to join together with parents to provide a consistent message to the child. Maizzie's mum saw us as part of the authorities: a nuisance and a barrier to her well-being. We tried hard to communicate our support and celebration of the pupil to their parents, but it did not always work.

One more typical feature of the visit was the dilemma I often felt regarding parents and carers. On the one hand, I needed to work with them in supporting the child. In this case, judging her mum may have caused tension in Maizzie's mind. However, it is equally possible that staying neutral may have made it appear to Maizzie that we were condoning parental actions which were clearly unacceptable.

We wanted Maizzie to be able to say what was really going on at home, but she never did. Many times I saw children who would have been far safer had they disclosed the abuse going on at home refuse to do so, because they could not countenance breaking the tie they had with their parents. Even when there is no such abuse, we have to recognise that while we may strive to empower children, our actions may cause them more difficulty than good. As Edelsky points out, a child who experiences a school discourse that validates their voice may feel tension when returning to a home environment that does not.[1] In my experience, this can lead children to reject the school discourse.

The past

Our behaviour is influenced by our emotions, which are closely related to our past experiences and the beliefs associated with them. Thus the past provides a context to our present, and can significantly affect the meanings that are made there. Charlie's story clearly exemplifies this. It began and ended with him sitting on a plush sofa in a well-appointed living room, patting a dog rather than talking to me. There were two different dogs, sofas and living rooms, and two different families who owned them, though they had in common a naïve belief that they were the people who would love Charlie better, that their love would be more effective than everything he'd had before, and that it would be enough to counter all that Charlie'd had to endure up to this point.

The first family were George and Sal, whose house was on a busy road leading into a small town. The noise from the traffic was absorbed by the cheap double glazing, the secluding lace curtains and the many trinkets that adorned the window sill. Charlie sat there, aged 13, trapped in the niceness of the furnishings, so far out of his comfort zone that he could not move. He had a pinched expression and was wiry and wary of eye, all of which made his smile and chuckle all the more charming when they appeared later. He was far from smiling on the first occasion we met. He did not know what to do or how to act. His only form of politeness was to sit quietly and keep his thoughts to himself. So I did all the work, asking the questions about how long he had been out of school, and discussing with George and Sal (who were keen to help give the conversation some legs to compensate for Charlie's monosyllabic replies) such issues as the long taxi ride Charlie would need to take every day to travel to and from our school. They weren't happy about it, but as the county they lived in had run out of educational providers that were

---

1 Carole Edelsky, *With Literacy and Justice for All* (London: Falmer, 1991).

willing to allow Charlie to attend, there did not seem to be any choice. George and Sal knew how limited Charlie's choices were; they themselves had agreed to foster him on a ten-day emergency placement, and that had been two years ago.

Charlie's paperwork gave little clue as to what he was like. It spoke of 'anger management issues', 'strong character', 'short attention span', 'communication difficulties' and the like. It was typical of the statements we received: generic and unhelpful. Such statements could mean anything from a child who had hated the demands of mainstream school but whose behaviour problems would evaporate once they settled into the more caring ethos and slower pace of a special school to a budding psychopath with a serious criminal career trajectory ahead of them.

Sitting there watching Charlie squirm was not helping me come to any conclusions. George interjected that Charlie would not mind the taxi ride, as he liked cars. Charlie's face was flushed as he nodded confirmation of this, but his eyes glazed over as George told what felt like a well-worn story about the time when Charlie had asked about the A1, the road that linked where Charlie lived now with his home town some 40 miles away. Charlie, George said, had one day asked where the road started and finished, so George told Charlie to grab his coat and off they went, driving all the way to the outskirts of London and back. George smiled at the memory, but I wondered if this had been a bit of an overreaction to Charlie's enquiry, possibly an overcompensation for the fact that Charlie asked so few questions. Also, perhaps Charlie had been not-so-secretly asking about his home town, where his family still lived. The social worker on the case had told me that they had deliberately moved Charlie as far away from his family as possible, as they were 'bad news', but I was guessing that Charlie did not see it that way.

Eventually Charlie was allowed to go to his bedroom, and George and Sal gave me their views more freely. They told me that he was a smashing lad – so polite – who was no bother really, apart from setting fire to the curtains in his bedroom a few times. Oh, and the bother they'd had at the start of his placement when they had found him being cruel to their severely disabled son. But that was all in the past, and now they just wanted him in school. They told me that he had been brought to them wearing nothing but a torn pair of trousers. He'd had no shoes, no shirt and no other possessions, although he was accompanied by the description *feral*, which at first they had not believed, but it turned out to be accurate.

Charlie's full name was Charles Edward George Henry, a regal name for one so mean of birth. Charlie had many of the traits that are common in unloved children. He had no real sense of himself. He was used to being discounted and had not learned to notice – never mind value – his own feelings and opinions. He often did not know what he felt or what he thought. As a person unhappy with their appearance may avoid looking in a mirror, Charlie preferred not to do any activity that could cause him to reflect on himself. He did not analyse his actions at all, and so had little sense of consequence. If he was heading for trouble, there was no executive decision-making that could get him to choose a different course. After joining us, he repeated arguments with his peers or with staff over and over; it never occurred to him to do things differently, because he had no sense of being an agent in the world. And if things went awry, this merely reinforced the fact that things always went awry, because that was the way of the world. Charlie was used to the fact that everything he touched turned to dust.

Charlie also had the curious relationship with truth that many troubled children have. Because they are emotionally immature, they have not got past the stage of thinking that theirs is the only consciousness. They lack empathy because they are not really capable of acknowledging the existence of other perspectives; their thinking is the only thinking. Other views which may challenge their own and which cannot be dismissed as stupid are seen as hostile, a personal affront. Not only does this make educational activities such as debating or discursive writing impossible, but it leads to the curious internal mantra of 'If I think it, it must be true', a belief which means that behaviour management becomes quite a challenge. The only way we were going to help Charlie's behaviour was if we could get him to think *about* it, without guilt or feelings of doom, but that became hard to do when Charlie's understanding was that if nobody saw him throw, hit or say what he threw, hit or said, *therefore he did not do it*. Actually believing this, rather than pretending to, meant that being accused of something was yet another personal affront, to be warded off with self-righteous verbal aggression.

Charlie's lack of empathy meant that he was incapable of friendship of any real quality and, like nearly all the children I have taught, he inhabited a very lonely world. There were times when his ignorance of others' rights or feelings was chilling. In one lesson, we were making a list of what he would buy if he had millions of pounds, and after he had exhausted his imaginary desire for Lamborghinis and private jets, he said that he would get his parents and brother something, but he did not know what. I pushed him to think about the other people who might be important to him, and what they might like, but he could not think of anyone else. I suggested he might like to buy his carers, George and Sal, something. He looked at me as though I had said something totally random and then continued with his own thoughts. So I pushed a bit more, and pointed out that they had looked after him for a couple of years now; did he have any desire to thank them for this in any way? This was again met with total indifference, and slight bemusement. Charlie's stay with George and Sal had engendered no sense of affection, loyalty, gratitude or even simple belonging in him whatsoever.

Perhaps the most common trait that Charlie shared with other troubled pupils was his attitude towards work. He had no work ethic at all. He did not like work, was not used to concentrating, tired easily, feared new things and ideas, and knew a range of strategies to avoid having any demands put on him at all. He did not like reading or writing because he could not do it, or so he thought.

Now I have some sympathy for pupils whose low self-esteem means they need a lot of reassurance just to feel barely adequate. They are bound to experience friction when they come into contact with a school system that rarely allows them to develop at their own pace. Charlie's experience of school was one of failure and rejection, and so it is not surprising that he had developed an alternative curriculum for himself. His way of getting positive regard did not involve the teachers, but the other pupils, whom he would try to impress with daring acts of impudence, abuse or barefaced defiance.

So it used to go like this: Charlie would come in to school happily and seek out one of the adults to chat to. He found adult company easy and gratifying. In adult company – once he had got to know the adult – he was charming and, above all, curious; he wanted to know how the world worked and chatted about it in a way that showed he was developing some sense of wanting to learn about life. Then it would be time for work, and Charlie would become slow to find a pencil, slow to sit down, and clearly on the lookout for any distraction. If the adult was not experienced in sticking to the agenda, Charlie would involve them in distracting chatter, or get them to pay attention to other, seemingly less engaged children. Failing all that, he would pick an argument with another pupil or with the adult themselves, and perhaps walk out of the class in righteous indignation at the way he had been treated. Basically, Charlie was as slippery as an eel when he first came to us, and this had a knock-on effect on all the other pupils. For Charlie, the best option of all was for him to catch a glint in another pupil's eye, a sign that they were up for making mischief. Then the silliness would start. Rubbers would be thrown, or silly noises made, and then, suddenly, the chairs and tables would be tipped over and off Charlie and whoever had joined in would run down the corridor, banging on other classroom windows as a sign of defiance as well as a call to arms for any other pupil who wanted to join in the fun.

Despite all of this, we did make progress with Charlie. We stopped him running around school by physically standing in his way and, more importantly, by building warm and caring relationships with him. He was easy to like as he was an effervescent character, and once he saw how he could channel his qualities in a positive way, he started to accept how we did things. He never quite lost his anarchic streak, but he actually spent a lot of time learning. He learned how to write his name and most of his address. He learned how to tell the time and to do some basic maths. He developed a knack for crafts – nothing that would win a prize in a show, but things that he could take pride in. He started to talk of his future with hope in his voice. He even looked down on newer pupils who tried messing about as a way of avoiding work. We followed everything up – the good and the undesirable – and slowly it began to seem that we were edging towards a miracle.

His transformation was not complete, however. Whenever he and I spoke in my office about his future, I would lay out all the positives – the feelings of pride and hope, and the sense of connection with others that he had earned for himself. If he was in the office for a transgression – a temporary relapse into his old ways – I would wait until the colour had faded from his cheeks, and the guilt and rage had subsided from his thinking, and say that he was at a crossroads: that he could choose the life of hope that he frequently (if a little unconvincingly) talked about for himself. For Charlie, the road to some kind of redemption from a past he did not ask for would be slow and steady. The pleasures and rewards on this road were great indeed, but they did not have the Dionysian attractions of the other road: the thrill of self-destruction.

These talks always worked in the short term, in that Charlie was returned to the straight and narrow. He would apologise to anyone he had hurt, and his humour and burgeoning work ethic would return. In the long term, however, I was never convinced. Whenever I asked him what he really wanted from his life – and whether he wanted to feel proud and positive, or to engage in activities that were exciting in the short term but would have more serious consequences in the longer term (Charlie had arrived at our school with the certainty that prison was his destiny) – his answer was always the same: 'I don't know.' Even when I came back at him with the idea that not knowing was the same as not deciding, which was the same as choosing the wrong path, he could not truly commit. And the more we got to know Charlie, the more the reason for this became clear.

Charlie's brother had been his main carer while he had been at home. His mum was not able to care for him. She had learning difficulties, and did not understand how to look after herself, never mind others. Charlie's dad had flitted in and out of his life. Charlie's favourite, possibly only, story about his father was about the time when the front door burst open and in he ran. As he disappeared upstairs, there were the sounds of the police arriving at the garden gate. They ran in and followed him upstairs. Charlie described the frantic footsteps and voices up above, then how everything slowly quietened down and how eventually, presumably reluctantly, the police came downstairs without their man. They talked briefly to Charlie and his brother, asking where their dad had gone, obviously confused as to where he could be. They were just about to leave when the sound of a massive fart rang out above their heads. The police ran back upstairs and found Charlie's dad squashed between the plasterboard and the bricks in the wall of one of the bedrooms. His dad was taken off for another spell in jail, but Charlie could only, it seemed, see the funny side of this story.

It dawned on me that, for Charlie, the thrill of committing misdemeanours had a contingent emotion intertwined with it, and that was the thrill of intimacy. That was why Charlie had wanted to run around school – it had been his way of feeling close to his fellow pupils, if only for a brief but intense moment or two. And when Charlie talked about his brother, who was seven or eight years older than him, his stories were always about 'jobs' they had been on, such as breaking into the local cricket pavilion or stealing from shops. Charlie's most treasured memories were of intimacy mixed with wrongdoing: the thrill of it was what bound him to others.

Charlie's brother was in prison and had been for a long time. He and Charlie shared the same social worker, who was always at pains to point out to Charlie that she did not want to talk to him about his brother. She explained to me that this was because his brother was categorised as highly dangerous within the prison, and also because he showed absolutely no interest in Charlie. Charlie's dreams of a reunion somewhere down the line were his alone. His brother was only interested in having Charlie along for jobs in the past because of Charlie's small stature, which made him ideal for being pushed through skylights and other narrow gaps so that he could unlock buildings from the inside.

We continued to get Charlie to make progress but then along came Tracy, an uncared for and often uncaring girl. She was in the year group above Charlie and one day she told him that he could be her boyfriend. One of six children, Tracy had a moral code that was regularly breached by the exigencies of poverty, and erratic and explosive attachment patterns within her own family. Charlie's emotions were suddenly all over the place, so we spent some time helping the new couple learn the basics of being nice to each other. It would have been simpler if the relationship did not happen, of course, but that was not an option. Charlie found the idea of someone selecting him as a friend immensely seductive, and why shouldn't he? Tracy had a sensible side to her and at times kept Charlie in check. But the turbulence of the relationship stirred Charlie up and made it difficult for him to think about his future. Rather, he went back to being driven by the invisible forces of the emotions that had shaped him so far: his feelings towards a family that did not exist, and his mistaken intuition that the excitement of criminal activity could once again prove a bond between him and his brother.

We carried on, and Charlie carried on learning. He even managed to concentrate long enough to learn to spell the name of his town, which was 13 letters long, using mnemonics to guide him through. He started going to work experience and new classes (as opposed to staying within the unit) and talking to a much wider range of people with a newfound confidence in himself. He was a changed man. Or so it almost seemed. There were still moments of giddy anarchy, followed by brooding anger or depression. He still said, 'I don't know' when asked what he really wanted from his life. Charlie knew that when his brother next saw him, he would barely want to recognise the person who Charlie had become if he could read, reason and take responsibility for himself. This thought lay heavy on Charlie's shoulders.

I worked hard on flooding Charlie's mind with the positive thoughts that could lock him into a virtuous circle of achievement leading to greater pride leading to even greater achievement. It felt like we were doing too much of the work, sometimes pushing Charlie further towards that circle than he himself wanted to go. But he asked for the pep talks and the reassurance. He wanted someone with the experience and the imagination to lay out a different future to the one he had foreseen for himself. Well, at least part of him wanted it.

When I went on a five-day training course, Charlie waited until the final day of my absence before making his move. My colleague said that she knew something was amiss on that final day when he arrived at school with his CD player and his hat – his only valued possessions which he never brought in for fear of getting them dirty or damaged. After a day of whipping other pupils into joining him in disruption and anarchy, he climbed a tree in the grounds of the school and refused to come down. When it was pointed out to him that he would have to come down eventually, he changed his message to his intention of never going back to George and Sal's, and of never coming back to this school again.

There are many very good reasons why social workers are taught to respect the voice of their clients. They need to ensure that they have their clients' interests at heart. It is easy to imagine that the supposed good deeds which are done *for* someone or, even worse, *to* them are not always perceived this way by the person themselves. So making sure the client has a voice and that it is heard is important. But there was an argument for the social worker to not accede to Charlie's requests or demands. Surely this was a case in which to say, while we hear what you are saying, you perhaps do not know best in this particular situation? And then to suspend all decisions until everyone involved has talked everything through. Well, perhaps there was a case for this. I was not party to any of those discussions. All I knew was that when I returned from my course, Charlie was no longer there, and the social worker was now fitting her narrative about Charlie into the new situation. This new carer would be good for Charlie because she had a 16-year-old son, so obviously knew the ropes when it came to handling teenagers. They would find a new school; perhaps the local mainstream school was worth a try?

And so it was that I went round to another house in the suburbs, where Charlie was sat on another sofa, preferring to pat another dog rather than look me in the eye. I introduced myself to his new carer before going into the living room. The carer was very sweet but was convinced that I, and his previous carers, fell into the category of 'part of the problem', whereas she was clearly 'part of the solution'. When I went in to talk to Charlie, he was shut down and I realised that I had little or no authority here. I was merely embarrassing him. The flush in his cheeks was back, along with the guarded look.

As I drove away, having got absolutely nowhere, I felt an array of emotions. I felt sad for Charlie on a personal level, but there were 16 other children in my care at school who still needed as much support and attention as I could give them. I felt sad that, yet again, I'd had to ask a child to make a choice, rather than the system taking enough care of him not to demand some miraculous leap of faith from a child who had such little faith in the first place. I also have to admit that I felt a bit of relief. The two and a half years with Charlie had been an intense time, and if it was to end like this, then so be it.

The social worker reported a few months later that Charlie was doing well in his new placement – following yet another upheaval – a children's home with five other boys who had similar problems. My heart sank at this news, as the last thing Charlie needed was to have his emotional and behavioural world shaped by living with other emotionally disturbed children. Then news of the trouble he was getting into started to filter through. He was shoplifting with one of the boys. He was caught after setting fire to a barn with Tracy, a barn which had belonged to Tracy's uncle. That was the last I heard of Charlie. A few days after he left our school, I got a distraught call from Sal, who had always tried her best for Charlie and couldn't understand his total rejection of her and George; he even refused to allow them to go round to take the rest of his few belongings and say goodbye. I tried to tell her the rejection was because she, like us, had held up the promise of success for Charlie, and he could not cope with that idea, but she wasn't buying it.

Chapter 4
The learner

The permutations of unhappiness seem to be infinite. Even after three decades of working with troubled children, I know there is a good chance that the next pupil through my door will still catch me by surprise. Every new unhappy pupil brings a new manifestation of unhappiness, a new iteration of the puzzle. There seem to be exceptions to almost every rule. For example, after all that I have said about underachievement, I have met a few children who have, I suspect, become good at learning *because* of their unhappiness. Ronnie, for example, responded to the trauma he had experienced by trying to build up his intellectual powers so that he could make the world safe by understanding it, and stay in a position where he had the power to retain control. He, perhaps rightly, used to boast to the staff at his school that they were not his intellectual equals. He was incredibly well read, and he coasted to a very good grade in his maths exam. But there was still something about his intelligence that seemed in deficit. He had a rather cold and unempathetic way of thinking. After he left us, he went on to spend some time as a collector of debts for a bookie. Not only did he have the mathematical skill to renegotiate debts at favourable interest rates, he was also happy to produce a baseball bat out of the back of the car when circumstances called for a little cold persuasion.

Because the varieties of unhappiness are too numerous to catalogue, this chapter does not attempt to do so. Instead it focuses on four key themes. Firstly, we consider in more detail the idea that behaviour is a communication of unmet need. The second focus is egocentricity, one of the few common characteristics that troubled children share. Thirdly, we look at the relationship between power, control and anxiety. And finally, we look at how troubled children may lack even the foundations on which to develop the productive learning that they need to experience.

Behaviour as a communication of unmet need

Getting our needs met is a primary motivator in our lives, and, as such, it shapes our behaviour. If we are hungry, we will do what we can to eat. Depending on our degree of hunger and the circumstances, our way of satisfying that need will be more or less respectful of the needs of others. On one trip to a local swimming pool, I once had to physically restrain a boy because he was so intent on stealing a piece of flapjack from the counter of the on-site café. When I later encouraged him to explore what all the consequences of stealing would be for him, I asked him, 'Geoffrey, what *were* you thinking?' He replied, 'I was thinking how sweet that flapjack would taste as it melted on my tongue.'

As it is with hunger, so it is with all our other needs. There are many theoretical models of needs, the most famous of which is Maslow's,[1] but I prefer those which portray a person's needs as a wheel. This is the image that I have in my head when I envisage the needs of most of the children I teach:

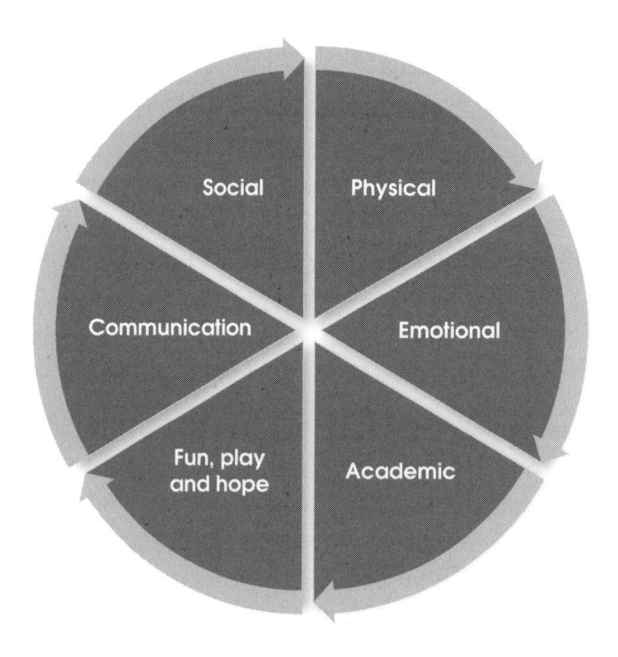

---

1   Abraham H. Maslow, A Theory of Human Motivation. *Psychological Review*, 50(4) (1943): 370–396.

At times, the segments may vary in proportion to reflect their relative importance, or even taken on different titles, depending on the context. And I include *fun, play and hope* to stop the whole thing becoming too clinical. The salient point is that if any segment is insufficiently developed, the wheel cannot keep turning. It would be nice to think that we can help children whatever their needs are. If they are hungry, we find them food; if they struggle to understand a maths problem, we break it down into manageable chunks, and so on. It seems a straightforward process, until we come to trying to meet their emotional needs. Then the problem gets more complicated.

It gets complicated because we are not always good at identifying emotional needs. I have limited skills when it comes to recognising my own, let alone those of others. For example, while I have learned that late morning grumpiness is usually a sign that I am hungry or tired, there are many occasions when I am not so perceptive. Recently, I had an argument with a coach driver while travelling in Europe. Half an hour later, when my wife said that she could see I was starting to calm down, I was surprised. I thought I had maintained admirable poise and calm throughout the incident. But it turns out that I am not as adept at reading my emotions and responding to them as I thought I was. This is true of many adults. If we could all identify accurately and respond appropriately to our emotions, life would be much simpler. We would have fewer dramas in life and fewer soap operas on TV.

There is a complicating factor that we need to address. We know that troubled children come into school needing to manage their emotions, and because this task is often beyond them, they need someone to do it for them. Their levels of loneliness, sadness, anxiety, depression and anger often overwhelm what few resources they have. Of course, if they came in holding a placard that stated the nature of their suffering – or communicated this is any similarly obvious way – we would rush to help. We would comfort and nurture them as a matter of course.

Unfortunately, that does not happen. We do not often get presented with an understanding that we can buy into immediately. This could only happen if the child had a well-developed ability to assess and analyse their own emotions, and clear ways of communicating this to adults who may not themselves be adept at listening. It seems obvious to state that if the child were able to communicate these emotions accurately, then they would be playing an active part in creating shared meanings, their needs would be met more easily and there would be less chance of challenging behaviour occurring. Sadly, as I have already said, we are dealing with children who have a reduced ability to create shared meanings but a greater than average need to do so. If we are going to help them, we need to be skilled at interpreting their behaviour. They are effectively asking us to understand them for them. Skilled parents do this all the time for their children. We should be able to do this in school for our pupils. Sadly, some schools do not seem to think it important, and meet challenging behaviour with punishment and anger.

I recently asked a young mother how her child was settling into his reception class. She told me that he loved it, although he often got upset at being demoted from green to orange on the behaviour management system. This was because he was slow at getting up from the carpet and going to work at his desk, which in turn was because he has mild cerebral palsy. This is just one anecdote, and I cannot comment on how often this type of thing happens in schools across the country, but we need to make sure our practice does not fall into similar traps. The staff supporting Geoffrey, the boy who wanted to steal the flapjack, for instance, had forgotten to take his snack to the pool that morning.

Even when the will to identify a child's needs accurately is there, it is sometimes a complex challenge to do so. Take, for example, Maizzie, who I introduced in Chapter 3. Her challenging behaviour one day turned on her friend, Lydia. Lydia was a gentle and warm girl whose friendship provided Maizzie with a haven away from all her worries and dark thoughts. Lydia was from a minority ethnic background, and had had major brain surgery, which had left her skull vulnerable to trauma. On a number of occasions, Maizzie used racist language towards Lydia, while threatening to smash her head against a wall.

On the surface, the behaviour was racist aggression. That was certainly how Lydia's parents saw it when they burst into my office the day after the first incident, demanding Maizzie's instant expulsion from the school. And who could blame them for seeing it that way? We were in a very difficult position. We had a duty to keep Lydia safe but we also had a duty to help Maizzie, and this could only happen if we understood the motivations for such behaviour. Maizzie felt unable to protect herself from the abuse that she was in all likelihood experiencing at home. She felt unable to ask for help from others, and so there were times when her feelings overcame her, and her only option was to push what she felt was the most destructive button at her disposal. Talking to her about the gravity of using racist language was counterproductive. She had the egocentricity of the truly desperate, and that meant that we were asking her in vain to be empathetic, to appreciate the centuries of prejudice and discrimination that lay behind the word she'd used. A boy once said to me, 'Why should I care about others when no one cares about me?' and who could blame Maizzie if this was her attitude now? Trying to impress upon her the terribleness of the word she'd used was missing the point. Her desperation not only made her immune to the needs of others, it made her use the needs of others as a way of meeting her own needs. Maizzie was not racist, I believe. She just knew that that word was the most destructive one she could employ. It was pointless to ask her for care and consideration for others when she felt the need for destruction. There was no room for hope in her head for anything more positive.

Egocentricity

There are a number of causes of the unusually high levels of egocentricity among my pupils. Some come from households where the rule is everyone for themselves, and that selfishness is brought into the classroom. Others are just stuck at an emotional age at which egocentricity is a common feature. Some have had their needs ignored so much that they have the neediness of the truly desperate. Some are missing those early play and socialisation experiences that nudge us towards a recognition of others as people too. Some are wary of connecting with other people because of negative experiences they have had in the past. Some have mental health difficulties which make connection with others undesirable or hard to achieve. And, finally, there is the possibility of a condition such as autism, which makes appreciating the minds of others difficult.

Whatever the cause, the common effect of heightened egocentricity is that shared meanings are harder to engage in. Egocentric children lose out. They find it harder to be rational in their arguments because they do not do what the rest of us do; they don't test out their thinking by bouncing it off other people. They have no quality control, so they can get lost in their thinking very easily. They can be hoodwinked into thinking that shortcuts like aggression, sulking, selfishness and tantrum behaviours – and, later on, drug use, alcohol or sex instead of love – are the answers. If you never test your ideas in the crucible of dialogue, then you can become prey to faulty reasoning, hypocrisy, bias and so on.

All of the activities we do at school are based on sharing meanings. When we read, we need to share meanings with the author, and we need a sense of empathy to understand the people in the book, be they fictional or real. When we write, we need to appreciate the intended reader and their needs. Debating or discussing without an appreciation of others' minds descends into arguing and abuse. The lack of ability to engage in shared meanings can result in reduced powers of assessment and analysis. It can hamper a sense of truth, consequence and justice.

It is easy to see how egocentricity leads to a place where criminal behaviour may start. It can seem like a serious injustice for others to have what you do not, be that extra free time at the end of a lesson, a toy or a flashy car. And even if people get hurt along the way as you right that perceived injustice, your lack of empathy means that you are inoculated from consideration of their pain.

Of course, if you are very egocentric, then you are in a precarious position, because deep bonds are not available to you. You may form temporary alliances, but they are shallow, and easily broken if things do not go your way, so you live in a state of loneliness: a country with the population of one. Anyone who crosses the border into your state is a potential invader, and if they have traits that you cannot understand – such as a different cultural background or visible physical differences – then you keep clear, or keep a wary eye. Better still, because you want to get the situation sorted, is to go on the attack. And if you have suffered from neglect or abuse in the past, such an attack will have the added bonus of allowing you to discharge difficult emotions, at least for a short while.

Whatever the root cause of this egocentricity, the best remedy is always the same, and that is to give the egocentric child experience of rich, meaningful and positive connections. Rhys was a boy who seemed locked in by his autism. He spent two years bent on revenge on one of his former friends who, he felt, had denigrated his experience of being bullied. Rhys talked about coming into school one day and making everyone see just how powerful he could be. I asked him once, only half in jest, if he had a list of people who he would target if he ever had the power or the means to do so. 'Yes,' he said, 'and you are number 78 on it.'

Several years later, he had transformed himself. He was much more sociable, thoughtful and, above all, empathetic. I asked him what had made the difference. What helped him become a person who was able to connect more with others? He surprised me with his answer. He said that he had felt locked away for many years, unable to make contact with anyone. But he could pinpoint the time when all this changed. He said that it was when he was in Ms Hewson's class. 'There was just so much warmth in the class that year. I really was amazed at all the kindness that Ms Hewson and her team showed to us.'

Ms Hewson was a very warm teacher. She left two years before Rhys told me that he remembered her in this way. She left in part because she found the pain and suffering in her pupils' lives too much to bear. If I found her now and told her that her care had transformed one of her pupils' lives, I doubt that she would be able to tell which one I was referring to, because it was not as if she'd had particularly significant conversations, or the sense of a watershed moment, with Rhys. She was warm and caring to all the children in her class. This is something all teachers of children, troubled or otherwise, should remember and take heart in. The effects of the support given to a child may well only come out later in their lives, unseen by those who provided it. It may well come out when they are grown up and have choices to make about how they treat their own children, for example.

Power, control and anxiety

If a child is unable to engage in shared meanings, unable to connect with the people around them, they are in a position that seems to me to be unnatural. They are isolated at a time of life when the need for connection is perhaps at its greatest, given the need to learn the necessary knowledge and skills to become independent. These children are dependent on others and yet it is this very dependency that causes them difficulty.

Perhaps it is not surprising, then, that some children find replacements for, or alternatives to, the shared meanings that seem inaccessible to them. Martha, who joined us aged 13, initially seemed too innocent for our provision: her appearance and mild manner were not what we were used to. She had a sweet smile and wore her hair in pigtails. She took care to underline every heading in her exercise book, using implements from her treasured pencil case. She was always saying, 'Ooh, I'm really nervous!' to the extent that it became like her catchphrase. Her home life seemed chaotic, but she settled in well. Then one day she announced that she was going to marry Mr Brown, the head teacher. The other children laughed scathingly, but she was adamant. I pointed out that he was already married, but she dismissed that hurdle too.

It quickly became clear that she had similar designs on three other men. They were all in their fifties, had grey hair and were slightly full of figure, just like Mr Brown. One of these men was a newsreader on television. She had his picture on her bedroom wall. Another was a children's performer who she had seen on holiday. She waited outside the theatre every day after the performance, hoping for a glimpse of him. She had also looked up the telephone number of the theatre and used it to contact him, threatening to accuse him of rape unless he met with her. The third man was a neighbour, just a few doors down. Martha's family had to move her away, to her grandparents', because she kept going into his garden to spy on him, and even broke into his house to trash the living room. This was apparently because she realised that the police had been called about her, for which she blamed his wife. She broke in to vent her displeasure, not caring that the police were actually standing in the front drive at the time. I still have a scar on the back of my hand as a result of one of my attempts to get her to (from my point of view) see sense, calm down and seek more healthy connections with others.

There are other, less dramatic ways in which children try to take control over the nature of their interactions with other people. Imelda, for example, simply assumed that she always knew best. When I first started teaching her, she interrupted at the start of each lesson, telling me that she knew all about whatever subject we were learning about, and making comments that added nuance to the broad strokes of whatever I was saying. Trying to have a conversation with her was challenging. She filled the space between her and her interlocutor with her own words.

Millie did just the opposite. While her behaviour became ever more defiant, she would not – or could not – engage in any discussion or negotiation with us about what was driving the increase in challenging behaviour. It was like talking into a vacuum. When her behaviour got so violent that she was about to be sent home, we would lay it on the line. 'Look, you can either go to Mrs Hill (her beloved teaching assistant) when things are getting worrying and she will help you to calm down, or you can just carry on hitting. So, you can either stay in school or we will have to send you home. Which do you choose?' The answer was always the same: 'I don't know. You decide.' Whereas Imelda took control by seizing the whole of the agenda, Millie got her sense of control by never giving the adults anything to work with.

I have seen many other behaviours that are driven by a need to control the nature of the connection with other people. Here are just a few of them:

- **Obsessive behaviours.** Millie, for example, had selected several members of staff as people she wanted to be with (but rarely talk to). She had to touch their cars in the staff car park each morning. If they were not in their respective classrooms or offices, she would mess up their workspaces as a punishment.

- **Directing or bossing about other children.** See the example that follows of Kylie, who adopted the voice of the teacher.

- **Taking advantage of the staff's niceness.** By which I mean behaving in a way that they would not if they knew the staff would not be so forgiving.

- **Undermining adults and children, finding and exploiting their weak spots.** Jayden, who I'll introduce properly in Chapter 5, was an absolute master at finding exactly the right comment or action to trigger fear and confusion in the children and inexperienced staff around him. He seemed to have an intuitive grasp of people's emotions, and especially the areas where they were most vulnerable, even while seeming not to have any idea about his own.

- **Creating conflict between the people around them.** This is a method that has great attraction. Light the fuse and stand back to watch the fireworks.

It has the added advantage of being very easy to do in a classroom full of troubled children.

- **Playing staff off against each other.** If you do not get the answer you want from one person, keep asking around until you do.

- **Refusing to do something that they sense the staff want them to do, even if it is of benefit to them.** They want to maintain control, even if it leads to an outcome that is worse for them.

- **Assigning blame, judging or controlling the interpretation of situations.** For example, Ronnie usually interrupted me when I tried to talk to him about his behaviour, by saying things like, 'What you need to understand is that I am amazing, and it's irritating when people fail to appreciate that.'

- **Lying, or bending reality to fit their needs.** Shameless denial or 'wishful believing' can often get you a very long way.

- **Using subtle bullying in supposedly friendly interactions.** It is almost never 'just banter'.

- **Only eating certain foods.** This can be a way of demonstrating or maintaining autonomy.

- **Insisting that certain doors are shut, or that particular lights are on or off.** This might be to do with their sensory needs or because they find familiarity comforting, but there is certainly a control element involved.

- **Insisting that their view of reality is more important than anyone else's** – even if that means other people have to accept that they demand different things when they are in different moods.

- **Needing to know what is happening.** Unpredictability can be deeply unsettling.

- **Needing to stick to their routine.** Any departure from what's anticipated can cause distress.

The last two items in this list will probably be familiar to anyone who works with people with autism. Kylie, an 11-year-old girl with the condition, has a need for routines and to know what is happening. Her example illustrates a very important point about control.

If her arousal levels reach a certain state, Kylie will become extremely violent. Her chair-throwing really is out of control. Most pupils, were they to throw a chair in anger, would still retain some control. If there was a blind person in a wheelchair in the room, they would throw it away from them – they want to lash out, but they don't actually want to do harm. Kylie has no such control, so it is important to keep her calm. On one occasion when I was observing her class, she had just come in from playtime and was being left to eat her snack. Her voice started to rise in pitch and volume. She was admonishing the boy across her table, using phrases and intonations borrowed from the adults in the room. She was asked, and told, several times to quieten down, but this had no effect. Eventually someone brought over her schedule for the day, which is a strip of paper with pictures of the day's lessons and breaks stuck on it in chronological order. Kylie took hold of it greedily and went through the order, tapping each lesson obsessively in turn. Her mannerisms and voice softened. Disaster was averted.

Kylie's actions exemplify the point that behind control lies anxiety. Children who cannot feel the reference points that are provided by shared understandings are adrift in a sea of nothingness. What they want is to feel able to know where they are, where they are going and who is going to be there to help.

Kylie's mum said that she just tried to make Kylie feel happy by insisting that she was super special, the most important person in the world. She would greet her at the end of school every day with a new dress, satchel or other gift. She confessed to me that she had given Kylie so many presents, Kylie had lost count of what she had, and so her mum would often return them to the store the next day in exchange for the next present. But Kylie did not want to feel special, I believe. She wanted the sense of connection that comes with being part of a democracy, not the isolation of being a dictator, in control of everyone but trusting no one.

Shared meanings can provide the reassurance that Kylie sought, although her autism made these difficult for her to access. It is the same for any of us; democracy may be irksome because we must work to get along with others, but it is reassuring too. If I have a ten-minute conversation with someone and I do all the talking, and have not checked in with the other person about either their understanding or their opinion, I am left in the dark as to how much of a connection I have made. Whereas if we have a back-and-forth discussion, I am much more likely to feel that a connection has been made, even if we have had to agree to disagree on the topic we were discussing. Kylie's schedule, which locks her into her day, is a comfort because it gives her feedback and reference points.

Prizant asserts that anxiety underpins the need for control in children with autism.[2] He makes the vital point that the antidote to anxiety is trust. Trust is when you can know that shared meanings are available to you, and who they are available from, and how and when they can be accessed, and that above all they will be safe for you to enter into. Kylie's extreme behaviours clearly had the message, 'I need to trust in the adults, or I will take over myself,' and her way of doing that was very destructive. All the other controlling behaviours listed on pages 103–104 have similar underpinning messages. The answer is to give the controlling child the ability to trust, rather than enter into a battle to wrestle control back from them.

Structures and reference points – the foundations for learning

If children are egocentric and/or suffer from a lack of connection to others, there is a further barrier to their learning. Because they are not firmly connected to networks of communities, or to ways of thinking that accentuate the links and the relationships between them and others, they suffer from not having a secure sense of self in relation to the world. This means that their foundations for learning – having a clear sense of time, space and secure relationships with other people – are insufficiently strong, and so naturally their learning is impaired.

I started to understand this only after years of wondering about my pupils' poor sense of time and space, and themselves and their belongings. For a long time, I could not answer questions such as:

---

[2] Barry M. Prizant with Tom Fields-Meyer, *Uniquely Human: A Different Way of Seeing Autism* (New York: Simon & Schuster, 2016).

- Why do such a high proportion of them not understand the difference between a minute and an hour, or have the ability to judge roughly what a minute or an hour feels like in passing?

- Why do so many of them not understand maps, or have the ability to differentiate between cities and countries, or places which are near and those which are far away?

- Why, for crying out loud, do they not wear coats in the winter but have big puffer jackets on in the summer?

- Why are they almost universally poor at looking after their belongings?

- Why do some of them, no matter how much they are enjoying an activity, always interrupt it with the question, 'What's next?'

I have never been a tidy or particularly well-organised person, and that sometimes causes me anxiety. For example, when I lose my keys, my mood can dip wildly. My internal monologue goes something like this: 'You said you were going to be more organised, but you were not. It's not hard to do, to hang your keys up in the same place each time you come in, but you cannot even manage that. It's such a loser thing to do. And it's not just the keys, it's everything else in your life.' Then I find my keys, order is restored, and the intention to never let this situation happen again evaporates along with the negative feelings. However, it leaves me aware that there is a strong relationship between self, order and anxiety. When I have difficult situations to deal with, sitting down and planning what to do decreases my anxiety and helps me to feel better able to cope.

My pupils often have a poor sense of self and a dearth of structure in their lives. They make me look incredibly well-organised. I did not realise just how structured my life is until I started to make a list of the ways in which my identity is shaped, and my behaviour is modified, by the structures around me:

- **In relation to time.** I refer to clocks, watches, alarms, schedules for events (TV programmes, fixture lists, diaries, appointment reminders, calendars to remember key dates), routines for certain activities such as getting up, stipulations in my work contracts regarding working hours and breaks, travel timetables.

- **In relation to space.** I refer to maps, signs in public spaces, fences, paths, road signs, speed limits, knowledge of property rights, knowledge of direction, knowledge of units of measurement, borders and boundaries.

- **In relation to other people.** I refer to the rule of law, rules of etiquette, knowledge of non-verbal communication, guidance on working practices, democratic procedures, institution of marriage, highway code, wills, bank statements, tax returns, online social presence.

- **In relation to objects.** I refer to shopping lists, instruction leaflets, hire purchase contracts, the mantra 'a place for everything and everything in its place', alphabetised storage, contents pages, filing systems, recipes.

- **In relation to myself.** I refer to the sensory information produced by my body, weighing scales, knowledge of clothes and shoe size, qualifications, driving licence, passport, birth certificate, address, prescriptions, name and address of doctor, bank balance.

These are just a small sample of the things we may use in our lives to give us a sense of who we are and how to behave, and we can also consider less formal social and cultural reference points, such as fashion guiding our clothing or music choices, or newspapers guiding our opinions. We have routines that ease the flow of our daily activities, so we do not have to relocate or reinvent ourselves every time we get up or go to bed. When I want to eat, for example, I know which drawer the cutlery is in, and I even have it set out in the way that I think is right – from left to right, it goes knife, fork, spoon.

We are reliant on structure providing reference points in our lives to locate us in relation to the universals of space and time, and in relation to the specific people, customs, activities and objects that are familiar to us. Existence can be scary without such reference points. We are specks of dust in a vast universe, and we need a sense of who and what we are. Structure gives us shared meanings – jointly constructed reference points with which to fulfil this need.

The more confident we are about who we are, the more we can create or access structures which are appropriate to our needs. We need boundaries to guide us and make us feel safe. There is a transactional relationship between boundaries and anxiety. The fewer boundaries you have, the more anxious you will be. And the more anxious you are, the more difficult it is to access these boundaries because they are based on joint understandings of the world.

My pupils have far fewer of these reference points in their lives. They do not have the joint understandings that are part of the fabric of most people's lives, which allow us to know where we are in space and in time, and in relation to the other people and objects which help give us our identities. They do not have these reference points because of their egocentricity, and they live with a high level of anxiety, which only compounds the problem and makes joint understandings even more difficult to create. They have a limited sense of themselves and of the world as a result. There is overlap in this respect between troubled children and children with autism. There is an increased need when supporting both to use structure to allow them to feel locked into the world. It is hard to imagine what our lives would look like without the structures that we rely on so much, but to attempt to gives a window into what it must be like for these children.

Imagine if every time you left your house, you could not be sure that you would ever come back, or that the house would be there if you did. I once worked with a boy called Daniel who needed constant assurances about what was going to happen to him. Every time he started to get agitated, staff would calm him by reciting his agenda for the rest of the day: 'Daniel, you have got maths, then break, then English, then choose time, then circle time, then lunch, then play, then registration, then PE, then bus, then home, then tea with Mummy, and then TV, and then story, and then bed.' This had an instant calming effect.

Another boy, Toby, was astounded when his play therapist found him at the start of a new school year. He had moved classrooms and assumed that that meant they would never work together again. He could not believe that she had negotiated the vastness of the universe to find him again. His new classroom was next door to his old one. Toby once had to be restrained at a National Trust property he had visited with his class, as he had become violent when the class had to get back on the bus. The next time they went, the teacher gave Toby a timer to count down the forty minutes they were scheduled to be there. At the end of the thirty-ninth minute, the class came back to the bus and as the alarm beeped Toby got straight back on.

If there is little or no structure in your life, it is all too tempting to attach importance to the routines that seem to go on around you. Any changes, therefore, can provoke great anxiety. The opposite of anxiety is trust, and changes mean that trust is weakened. Teachers who work with children with autism or with troubled children will be familiar with the concept that if a member of staff is ill and has to be replaced by a supply teacher, the day has already become harder, even if the individual is familiar and good with the children.

The transactional relationship between structure and mental well-being does not just matter in the sense that the more you know about where you are in life in reference to time, space, other people and so on, the calmer you are likely to be. The systems we all use to understand time, place and relationships are themselves shared meanings, which provide the foundations for much of the communication of meanings that we engage in and rely on in our teaching and learning. Having a reduced ability to take part in the sharing of meanings does not just mean that conversations in the classroom are problematic; it often indicates that these underpinning understandings are not there.

We take many of the ways of structuring and imposing meaning on the world for granted, and we do not realise the importance of having shared meanings about what a minute or an hour is, or what north and south are, or what travelling a mile feels like. The way we structure our relationships is even less easy to access because it is less tangible – with fewer units of measurement – but the etiquette of interaction is nonetheless vital in ensuring that our engagement with others goes as positively as possible.

Working with troubled children led me to realise how vital such understandings are for learning. With a severely impaired grasp of these foundations, life becomes very difficult. While some of my pupils risk ending up in jail, many more risk ending up on their sofas, isolated not by the bars of a cell but by the attrition that they feel in their scant connections with the world outside their houses. Their lack of understanding of basic structures makes the world a difficult and often scary place. Of course, the remedy for this is for them to learn, but their ability to do that is severely impaired too because the fundamental understanding of time, space and connection with others underpins so much of what is taught and learned at school. The more you start to trust in the order in the world, the more you can buy into these concepts, and into the disciplines that we use to make sense of them.

Mathematics, physics, chemistry, history and geography help us to make sense of objects in time and space. The more you sense order in the social world – and the more you can see order in other people's understandings of the world – the more literature and the arts become vehicles for communicating deep emotions rather than meaningless marks on a page or canvas. Every lesson of every subject involves refining one's ability to understand, order and connect with the objects and people in our world. Without the knowledge and language of connection, there is no empathy, so characters in books never come alive, other people are never humanised, and the past and the future have no reality. Most subjects feel irrelevant, the domain of others. It is difficult to appreciate the relationships between elements or see the interconnectedness between ourselves and our environment. If you do not know how to use structures to make joint sense of time and space or to connect with other people, you start every lesson at a serious disadvantage. It really is miserable to have unsupported emotional problems as a child.

Chapter 5
Attuning to and containing emotions

Understanding that the emotions are a key part of the shared meanings in the classroom is not an end in itself. It leads to new understandings of the ways in which relationships work in the classroom. This chapter begins with a brief guide to some of these ways, and then looks in detail at a vital attribute of all productive shared meanings in the classroom: containment.

The less obvious roles of emotions in the classroom

Emotions are a guide, not a hindrance

Learning to manage my own emotions when dealing with challenging behaviour did not mean that I stopped feeling the difficult emotions. It just meant that I could use them as a way of interpreting what the child I was dealing with was feeling. Sometimes this was straightforward: in Chapter 2, I mentioned feeling lost when I dealt with Mark, only to discover that he too felt lost in the wake of the bereavements that had knocked him for six. With Millie, when I approached her because she was refusing to go into another lesson, I felt uncomfortable because I was experiencing anger at her refusal. I felt I should be more compassionate, as I knew just how much upheaval and rejection she had gone through in her short life. But one day she managed to use a feelings board to identify her emotions, and it turned out that – despite her smile, her shrinking posture and her refusal to talk – her predominant emotion was sometimes not fear but fury. With some children, I tell them about the emotions I feel and check whether they feel the same thing too.

Perhaps the most striking example of this reciprocity of feeling occurred when I started working with Jayden. Despite my own rule that you have to like the children, I found myself feeling dislike for him. I did not like the way he slouched, or the way the children and staff were scared of him. I found myself thinking that he was slovenly, a creepy kid with a weird haircut. I was very uncomfortable about this, but as I slowly got to understand the reasons behind Jayden's challenging behaviour, I realised that there were understandable (and perhaps forgivable) reasons for my feelings. Jayden was struggling with some very dark feelings. He felt that he was becoming, as his father had become before him, hostage to paedophilic urges and actions. This is why I had found him hard to like at the outset of our relationship. I had worked with children with sexualised behaviours before, but Jayden detested and feared this quality so much, he was giving off a disgust with himself. Once I understood this, I was able to work with him more effectively.

Attunement and the abyss

This kind of analysis, in which you monitor your own emotions to see if they are attuned to the child, only works if you are actually feeling the emotion with them. There is no shortcut. It is not possible to rationalise that a child's history must cause them anxiety, and so deal with the anxiety in a matter of fact way. It would be easier if we were dealing with fact rather than feeling, but if you want to maximise your connection with and understanding of a child, you have to be alongside them, feeling what they feel. This is tiring work. What makes it even more demanding is that there always seems to be a moment in the troubled child's relationship with the school when the future looks really bleak. Things often get to a place in the unit where there is going to be some sort of disaster, such as a breakdown in the child's placement.

Virtually every child we admitted into the unit for children with EBD followed the same pattern, whatever the nature of their disruptive behaviour. They took things right to the edge, they pushed us to the point where we felt we could not cope much longer. The violence was too much to tolerate, or the disruption too upsetting. Then they were either threatened with exclusion or were temporarily excluded for a few days. At that point, almost all of them reduced the level of intensity of their behaviours and settled down into working with us. Of course, you could explain this away with the idea that children need to know where the boundaries are, and that exclusion taught them a lesson, but I believe the real picture is more complex. I think they needed to look into the abyss – and have someone look in with them – before they could withdraw from the edge. It's as if they want you to know that they could have jumped, and want to know for themselves what it would have felt like. Or perhaps they wanted to test your faith in them, if faith is belief without a rational basis.

Having a crisis? Get in line

A colleague once said to me that our school was like a vending machine. As soon as you remove a chocolate bar from the front of the shelf, another one falls into its place. By that he meant that as soon as you resolve the issues of the pupil who is demanding all the attention and resources at a given moment, another pupil starts to become just as big a disruption. The explanation for this phenomenon, I believe, is that children do not take their problems to just anybody. They may not know it, but they are looking for people who can and will empathise, make them safe, acknowledge their needs and, above all, not shut them down with tellings-off that demand that they put the needs of other people first. So if you want to be someone who really helps children, you have to keep a line of communication open no matter what they throw at you, or how many victims are created along the way.

They don't want a disciplinarian who will judge them from on high, but neither do they want a bleeding heart to sympathise with them. They want someone with the strength and kindness to cut through any bullshit they (in their upset and confusion) might throw around. They want you to make it right. So if you are the type of person who can build the space that allows them to come to you, they will. In fact, they will flock to you.

They will flock because there is a lot of misery out there. There seems to be far more children with EBD in the system than we have resources to help. So if there are many children who need extra support and you happen to be someone who they can come to, why don't they all come knocking on your door at the same time? Why do they align themselves in a queue, like the chocolate bars in my colleague's vending machine analogy?

In my theory, the answer is that they know that if they all came along at once, there would be chaos. For many of the children I have taught, their chief way to communicate their problems was through disruption, subverting the normal flow of things. This took many forms, from throwing chairs to destroying their work, petty hatreds, incessant squabbling and so on. But the strangest thing was that, while they wanted to disrupt, they did not want to disrupt too much. What they could not afford to do was let this disruption turn into anarchic catastrophe. They knew where the edge of the abyss was. They also knew that they loved being with us, and loved getting the help we could give them; they just needed to know how much help was on offer. If one child went into crisis, and their needs increased, the other children never joined in to create a sense of anarchy, even though on a day-to-day basis any observer would have judged many of their actions as anarchic. If one child really went into meltdown, the others responded by becoming model citizens for a while. They knew that if they kicked off as well, they risked us all going over the cliff, so they counterbalanced the actions of the child in crisis with their own good behaviour. In this job you are always on the edge of an abyss, but somehow you never fall in. Even if there are times when faith is all you have left.

The micro and the macro

Sinason states that in a first therapeutic meeting, a child will communicate everything that the therapist needs in order to understand them and their reaction to the problems they face.[1] Given that the therapist and the teacher of troubled children have the same aims – to connect with and attune to the child in order to understand how they are thinking and feeling – the same should be true of the child in the classroom. If you look closely enough, you can see the nature of the bigger picture in the details. For example, Imelda (mentioned in Chapter 4) filled the space between me and her with words. She claimed superior knowledge, but in fact her understandings were superficial and dressed up. When I used some behaviour management techniques to frame her contributions as interruptions

---

1   Sinason, *Mental Handicap and the Human Condition*.

rather than as welcomed pieces of advice, she shut down. I could not get the right balance; she seemed to want the whole of the agenda or none of it.

Her behaviour on a more general level replicated what we saw in the classroom. Over the next two years, she went through a series of crises in her life that seemed to be part of a narrative that only she had a role in. When we met to discuss these crises, her tears were all-consuming. She said that she had been diagnosed with *schizophremia* [*sic*]. It turned out that there had been no such diagnosis. Nor were there diagnoses of autism, porphyria or becoming invisible, although fear of all of these had caused significant downturns in her mood. There was talk of suicide at one point, and also accusations that the head teacher of a previous school had raped her.

We addressed all of her claims seriously through the correct channels. We felt, however, that we too had a significant role to play in Imelda's well-being. While we could not offer psychotherapy or any such intervention, we tried to get her to see that connecting with other people in lessons was a kind of therapy in itself. It would do her good to share the agenda and to take part in discussion and debates, rather than tell everyone what her opinion was and then opt out. Education would help her to appreciate other viewpoints, broaden her horizons, help her to achieve and also to feel part of a community. We tried to dislodge her from the belief that we did not have the capacity to understand someone as complex as her. The final crisis she had was when she revealed that she was a boy in a girl's body. This was either the real underlying problem, which had taken some time to be revealed, or just another, very effective, way of monopolising the narrative.

The reason why it is possible to see a link between the minutiae of classroom life and the direction a pupil's life may take is because they come from the same root, which is the core beliefs of the pupil. Understanding this can be enlightening but it can also be worrying. You can never be sure, but sometimes you can witness behaviours or attitudes that could play out in a more serious way in the future, perhaps when there are no teachers or other containing or restraining forces around. For example, Richard was quiet most of the time, but would occasionally become very overexcited and giddy, often meaning that he both deliberately invited the derision of his peers and became intensely angry at that derision.

One day he came in to my classroom aggrieved because he had asked the head teacher to sign his application for a shotgun licence, and the head had, of course, refused. I pointed out to Richard that while he was normally a sensible chap, when he got overexcited, he could act rashly, and what would he do if he got very silly or into one of his rages with a shotgun in his hand?

'I would never shoot anyone, though, Sir.'

'Even if they were really picking on you?'

'No, no way. Well, not unless they deserved it.'

Richard never did get a shotgun, but he was involved in a terrible traffic accident several years after he left school. I look back on his behaviours, and those pupils who I know have gone on to commit acts of violence against themselves or others, and I wonder if we could have done more in terms of identifying and addressing certain behaviours and the sadness that lay behind them.

Teaching as therapy

As I've already stated, I realised early into my career that I was working with children whose ability even to read and write seemed compromised by their emotional difficulties. One example was Stefan, a boy who had experienced physical abuse, and who seemed to have protected himself from the consequent trauma by developing a chaotic way of thinking. He could spell out the words on the page very easily, but he could not get sentences to make sense. The subject would change mid-sentence, or the verb tenses would switch around, causing confusion in the reader. I found myself asking what the hell I was doing banging on about grammar to a child who clearly had more important issues on his mind. Should he not get therapy first, so that he could become able to deal with the trauma which muddled his thinking? Then would his reading and writing sort itself out?

It took me a while to realise the answer, which is that because the relationship between the emotions and cognition is a transactional one, Stefan's problem could be approached from both directions. Therapy would allow him to begin to untangle his emotional state, which would help him to think more clearly. But it was equally true that when we are teaching a child to think in more advanced ways, we are giving them the tools to deal with their emotions too. In this case, encouraging Stefan to empathise with his audience, to use writing to make sense of his world and to discover his own voice was tantamount to helping him develop emotional sense-making tools.

The complexity of the relationship between thinking and feeling

Much as though we may like to think of ourselves as capable of making wholly rational decisions, perhaps our emotions play a greater role than we realise, or are prepared to admit. For example, are our political views solely the product of rational analysis, or are they sometimes affected by the need to feel angry, or by a need for control, which is itself unconsciously driven by anxiety? Troubled children can show extreme overlap between feeling and thinking. Millie, who I've mentioned several times, seemed unable to protect herself from the emotions of others. She was unable to rationalise that a fellow pupil's pain or anxiety was not hers, and consequently had no mechanism for moderating her empathy. She would report being hurt even in circumstances in which she had been doing the hurting.

Jack, who I introduced in Chapter 2, experienced thoughts and emotions that lived together like bits of coloured paper in a kaleidoscope. A single stray thought could trigger all his anxieties, which, because he could not think them through, all tumbled into each other. One day a teacher praised him for completing his story plan, and said that he could choose to write about his own ideas or the ones suggested on the board. The choice was just too much, and he stormed out of the classroom. When, hours later, he was calm enough to allow us to think through all his worries with him, events from years back came pouring out, as they always did after such a crisis.

On another occasion, he looked for me at the start of the school day. He clung on to me (which was a little awkward as he was over six feet tall) and said that he had seen a woman with a cola can in her eye, and that there had been blood everywhere. He found it hard to think of anything else. I phoned Diana, his foster carer, who rather tiredly explained that Jack had been at a summer fair and had walked past an exhibition by a St John Ambulance team: one of the fake casualties was a woman who had a cut by her eye. I went back and reiterated this to Jack, and Diana and I explained it again together at a meeting the next day. Each time we talked it through, Jack nodded and smiled, clearly accepting our explanation for the moment. But his mind would not let it go. He continued to fret over it for several weeks. Every time he got worried, it was one of the things that percolated up to the top of his thoughts, but his ability to rationalise such thoughts was insufficient to deal with the emotional impact they had on him.

No one is neutral, and no one stops learning

While it is important to be as strong, open and objective as possible, so that troubled children can relate to you, it is also important to acknowledge that sometimes such a stance is difficult to take. We are all human, and we need to be aware of our limitations, our biases and our own needs.

Working with troubled children is hard work and is often not very well-paid, so it is not really the type of job that people drift into by chance. It is important to recognise one's own reasons for being in this line of work. People have their own agendas, of course. For example, I feel I am there for reasons that almost certainly relate to my own childhood. My parents divorced when I was ten, and although as traumas go it was probably less to deal with than anything my pupils have had to endure, it was still my trauma. I spent a lot of time and energy looking for a father figure after the divorce, and this probably had a bearing on my career choice. Or perhaps I simply wanted to find out about how my own emotions worked. It is certainly true that teaching about the emotions has meant that I have learned a lot about myself. I am not sure which explanation is the most relevant, but it is not vital to find a definitive answer to the question about why you are there. It is more important just to consider the question, and to acknowledge one's own capacity for bias.

Containment

A teacher who is proficient at teaching a class of troubled children will have in place a variety of effective strategies. They may have thought carefully about the geography of the classroom, so that they can see everything, or so that the children are facing the teacher more than they are facing each other. The catalyst child, the one who sets the others going, may be positioned close to the teacher. The teacher may well have developed the art of being able to write on the board while facing the children. They may be able to predict when someone is about to lose concentration, and are able to change the flow of the lesson accordingly. They will know which activities tend to lead to conflict and which don't. They will reframe minor transgressions into positives or teaching opportunities (for example, by saying, 'Well done for such an interesting answer, I can see that you are really thinking. Now let's see if next time you can do even better by putting your hand up first.'). They may have a bank of strategies up their sleeve to avoid giving the pupils the opportunity to refuse to do what they are being asked (see the advice on de-escalation in Chapter 6).

Each teacher will have their own style, but the one thing that defines every good classroom is the ethos of care that is present. It would not be long before any observer saw that here is a teacher who respects every pupil, knows them each inside out, is usually one step ahead of them, and is able to cope with anything that a pupil may throw at them, no matter how painful or disruptive these feelings or behaviour may be. The teacher is there, present in the room, for the children. They are gently but clearly able to lead the children to the next steps of their learning, and therefore there is a palpable feeling that the teacher will be there and the pupil will be all right. This is containment, whereby the teacher ensures that the shared meanings created in the classroom are bordered and safe.

Containment has many aspects to it. Children need to know that they are physically safe; we are trained to use physical intervention, such as restraint, to achieve this. They also need a moral and social framework. They need to know that if they have difficult emotions – from momentary embarrassment at not knowing the answer all the way to the most difficult feelings linked to previous trauma – the teacher will help them through the crisis. Containment is stepping in, whenever and wherever children have an unmet need. What follows are a few examples of containment in action.

Facilitating social interactions

In one unit for troubled children in which I worked, we had problems with fights and arguments at break and lunchtimes. We would keep children in as a consequence of their aggression. This led to what I assumed at the time to be unavoidable arguments with pupils who felt that we were being unfair, because they had not started the fight or felt they were the one being picked on. I did not see that we were repeatedly putting the children in an uncontained situation.

Then one day, Ashraf, a boy who caused many of these fights due to being an expert wind-up merchant, did something that made me rethink our approach. He invited me to his birthday party, which was being held one Sunday at his house. I was the only member of staff to be invited. When I asked him who else was coming, he told me that all his friends were the other pupils in the unit (none of whom lived near him, so he only ever saw them in school). These were the very people who regularly exorcised their deep anger at his wind-up tactics by being verbally and physically aggressive towards him. I expressed some surprise at his and his mum's decision to have them all over to their house. Ashraf explained blithely that he realised that there might be trouble, which was why I had been invited too, so I could keep the peace.

This made me think about break and lunchtimes. Why were we turfing these children out into the frenetic playground with minimal supervision and then getting surprised and disappointed when problems arose? So we changed the role of the staff out on duty during breaks. They now had the sole task of facilitating play and good relations. Meanwhile, we also put into place a risk assessment scheme. A pupil could go out only after 48 hours of calm behaviour. If they were aggressive, they had to stay in (supervised, but unpunished) until they had once again proven that they could be calm and were worthy of a degree of trust. We explained the scheme to the pupils by saying that they had to be kept safe, so we had to assess the risk. They accepted this, even the aggressive ones. It made perfect sense to everyone. So, actually, we changed almost nothing in terms of staffing or the number of children being kept in or let out, but there was no sense of anyone losing control of themselves, or of recriminations or punishment. As soon as we stopped expecting children to do what we knew they couldn't manage – and set ourselves up to manage relationships positively – the stress levels went down considerably, and everyone felt safer. This gave us time to follow up on the more minor disagreements, or intervene in arguments before they got nasty, so that we could do more teaching and less managing of crises and mopping up of blood.

Using containment within the family dynamic

The next example is of Janice, the mother of one of our pupils, who came to see me because her son, Scott, was driving her up the wall, or rather into the bathroom. Janice had recently got to the point where she could no longer bear Scott's behaviour, and would lock herself in the bathroom, swearing tearfully at him from behind the door to try to make him go away. Scott would stand outside, repeating the behaviour that his mum found so difficult to cope with. He kept saying that he had a tummy ache, over and over, with an increasing sense of desperation.

Scott was a 10-year-old with autism, who had been through a difficult time. He was not good at identifying his emotions or at differentiating between physical pain and discomfort and strong emotions such as anxiety, disappointment or excitement. He needed someone to help. Unfortunately, his mum found it difficult to fulfil this role. 'The thing is,' she said to me, 'I'm good at being a mum usually, and I am good at putting boundaries in. But I have no idea how to stop him doing this, and he is doing it more and more.'

While shutting yourself in the bathroom to get away from your child is not a recommended parenting technique, there was a reason, and I had no cause to doubt her claims about being a good mum. Scott had endured a series of major operations on his heart over the last few years, followed by a cocktail of serious medication. They had even experienced several crises: highly concerning setbacks in his treatment. It had been a difficult journey for all concerned. Now, the crisis was over but although the doctors had seen fit to give the responsibility for Scott's health back to her, she found it difficult to feel any sense of control, so harrowing had the journey been. When Scott was genuinely ill, he was a model patient: quiet and compliant. But Janice had had to listen to so many doctors' opinions, and witness so many severe fluctuations in Scott's well-being, that she could not really trust her own judgement any more. So when Scott came to her seeking to be reassured about his health or his worries, she could not give him what he wanted, which in turn made Scott even more anxious.

We made a plan. Janice took Scott for a thorough medical check-up, and once she had established that he was physically fine, she stepped up. She found ways of being resilient about Scott's state of health and started to contain his worries. We devised planned responses to Scott's statements, so that Janice could stick to a script that helped her to feel calm. So, for example, if Scott said that he felt ill on the way to school, Janice would refer to the social story they used which explained the protocol for what happened next. The story went like this:

> If I feel ill on the way to school, I will tell Mummy and she will listen to me and say that she will tell my teacher. When I get to school, the adults will listen to Mummy and keep an eye on me. They will phone Mummy at break to tell Mummy how I am. If I am still ill, Mummy will come and get me. I will tell Mummy about my illness once and then we will not talk about it anymore until Mummy tells my teacher.

Once this system was in place, Scott felt listened to, and because Janice felt calm and in control, he felt contained. He did not have to worry about his mum worrying any more. Janice had enough calm and space to slowly begin to rely on her intuition again when assessing Scott's physical state. Then his behaviour subsided very quickly.

Janice and Scott provide a neat example of containment because the aspect of Scott which needed containing, the area where he felt a lack in not only his own resources but in his mum's too, was quite specific. Usually children with EBD have a range of areas where they need support. They may need help with social skills, anxiety management, anger management, maintaining concentration, understanding consequences, empathy, accepting disappointment, understanding how to have fun safely, reading their own emotions, organising their stuff and so on.

Failure to contain

It is easy to fail to contain a pupil. If you fuss too much around an anxious pupil, emote too much around a pupil who is reserved, or panic around a nervous pupil, they will feel that they are not safe. It can feel unsafe if you are asking them for their opinion when they want you to provide the answers. You do not have to have all the answers, however; you just have to be able to appear calm even when you do not know what the answer is. A pupil can feel uncontained if their actions provoke difficult emotions in you – such as anger, anxiety or disappointment.

Containment can work at levels that are almost imperceptible. We once witnessed a sudden spike in extreme behaviour problems from Ahmed, a hyperactive boy. I could not understand why he seemed so anxious all the time, and why he seemed to be building a very unhealthy, almost obsessive dependence on one particular teaching assistant. Ahmed seemed almost unable to function without her. At the same time, her importance in his life was not enough to stop him regularly hurting her. Then she rang in one day to say that she was resigning. She had to give up her job because she was moving out of the area as a matter of urgency. She had just left her husband and needed to get herself and her children away from him, because he was physically abusing her.

Of course, the school was understanding – we wished we were aware of the situation sooner and could have done more to help – and supported her as best we could in this difficult time. However, her departure caused great anxiety among the class team, because they feared that Ahmed's behaviour would escalate even more now, such had been his dependence on her. It actually calmed and became acceptable and appropriate. It seemed that the teaching assistant's relationship with Ahmed had on some unconscious level left the door open to the possibility of him acting out when working with her, and he had walked through the door into behaviours that he himself did not particularly understand or feel the need to enact. When these behaviours were not shut down, or appropriate boundaries not put in place, this problematic relationship dynamic became more deeply entrenched. There had been an unfortunate matching up of their respective vulnerabilities, which meant that Ahmed's anxieties and consequent behaviours had not been contained.

There are many other ways that children can feel uncontained, including:

- If they have a worry that they are unable to share, or that the adults are unable to help with.
- If they are frightened by events in school, such as the threat of being bullied.
- If teachers seem too busy to notice their actions, whether positive or negative.
- If they get away with actions that they know they shouldn't.

Containment of serious behaviour

Jayden, who I've mentioned several times already, had a particular problem that led us to contain him in many different ways. When I first met him, he seemed to have very few boundaries; most of the pupils, and staff, were clearly scared of him. He was able to get under people's skin, find their weak spots and leave them feeling undermined and uncomfortable. He manipulated children, and frequently set them up against each other or against staff. It was not until we started to contain him that the reason for this behaviour became clear.

We tightened our monitoring of what went on in the playground. By having staff count the number of incidents of playfighting, we imposed our version of events over the children's claims that they were not playfighting, but just 'joking around'. Stopping playfighting reduced the number of subsequent real fights, and having calmer breaks removed the forum in which Jayden's manipulations usually occurred. I have already mentioned that I found Jayden difficult to like at first. But I managed to get past this – he had an emotional awareness that, when applied in positive ways, made him actually rather likeable – and from then on we had a meaningful mutual understanding. I suspect he could tell which staff were having to try their best, or pretending, to like him and knew that these were not the people he could go to for help.

Jayden often went out of his way to disrupt lessons, calmly but cruelly verbally attacking or making life awkward for any teacher or pupil who he perceived as weak. So we needed to contain his behaviours in class. We literally stood in his way and insisted that he stop. This drove him out into the corridor. When he was in the corridor, we again physically contained him, shepherding him into my office. Jayden's challenging behaviours had been his way of exorcising difficult feelings. Now his feelings had nowhere to go, so we started him with play therapy and made sure he had support from a teaching assistant who was an excellent listener.

In the office, Jayden would try to impose his meanings onto the agenda. He typically tried some crazed barrack-room lawyer shtick – for example, 'You told me to get off the table, but you did not say anything about not sitting on a pupil, did you?' He also tried shock tactics. On one occasion, when we were talking about life not being fair, I mentioned – as an example of unfairness – a nest of coot chicks which I had noticed one day while out walking. On the following day, they were gone, presumably predated by a fox or something. Jayden looked up from his slump and said, 'I'd have loved to have seen that, I'd have loved to have seen those chicks being ripped apart by a fox or whatever.'

I said, 'I'm sorry that life has done that to you, Jayden. I know how much you love animals and I am sorry that life has been so hard for you that you sometimes lose sight of what you really like and don't like.'

Jayden immediately looked up and started screaming at me, in howls of pain that he barely had the breath for.

'What's the point of being sorry? That's not going to change anything! It's not going to bring the chicks back! It's not going to change what my dad did or what I am, is it? No, it fucking well isn't!' And so on for the next few minutes until he subsided into pure sobbing. Eventually the energy for that ran out too.

The more we contained him, the more of these outbursts we saw. They came with a good deal of anger and self-pity, but neither of these feelings were at the core. What sat at the centre of Jayden's whole being was pure despair at what he saw as the all-consuming shame of being attracted to younger children. We did not ever force Jayden to confront the feelings behind his behaviour, but we couldn't help but confront his behaviours, which was tantamount to the same thing. He was never going to get a rollicking, but we had no choice but to get him to confront the problem that we had, which was a pupil taking serious chunks out of the positive ethos of a caring school. Jayden loved the caring aspect of school himself, but that in itself gave him a problem: it made him think about things. He could neither ignore his problems nor deal with them.

When Jayden was discovered abusing a younger child outside of school, the containment stepped up considerably. We had to contain him in school by putting into place constant supervision. We also started to work with a specialist team. They worked following the same principles as we did, seeing Jayden's behaviour as a communication of unmet need, and they worked to fulfil those needs so that the inappropriate behaviours would be redundant. This made perfect sense to me. I had worked with other children who had paedophilic tendencies, and they were all deeply traumatised. One had been removed from his house as a very young child when it became apparent to social workers that he was only able to sleep in his bed if he had a length of barbed wire with him for protection. By the time he came to us, he was at least six feet tall, but was mercilessly taunted by much smaller children, who sensed his vulnerability. Everyone scared him. He cowered from everyone except for very young children. Meeting a toddler gave him a seemingly irresistible opportunity to exercise power over someone else. I am not condoning such terrible behaviour, of course. What I am saying is that such behaviour always relates to unmet needs, like every other challenging behaviour.

The specialist team started to have a demonstrable effect on Jayden's life: his house was tidied, family relationships were restored, and his sister was dissuaded from the high-risk behaviours she had previously been involved in. But the most important change for Jayden occurred in his mum's attitude. The experts managed to convince her to see him not as a monster in the making – an inevitable copy of his father – but as a victim of his past, whose future was still up in the air, and whose sexual behaviours were unfortunate expressions of his needs, rather than milestones on an already determined path to becoming the worst kind of predator. There was, in other words, hope for him.

Once Jayden's mum accepted this different view of her son, Jayden's behaviour at school changed overnight. He was calm, happy to start to work in lessons (though years of refusal had significantly reduced his stamina and his ability to stick at a task). He even started to talk about his future. We built on this hope by putting in a personalised timetable to allow him to learn the skills he needed. But then the specialist team moved on. They left just before the summer holidays began.

Three days later, Jayden's mum bought him a phone – one that could take and send pictures. It was a responsibility that Jayden was not ready for, and he was again insufficiently contained. He sent inappropriate images to a girl. Lots of boys his age make mistakes like this, of course, but for his mum, all the hope and all the structures that had been put in place by the experts came crashing down. There was no longer anyone to advise caution before jumping to conclusions. She went back to the narrative of having known all along what Jayden would become.

Jayden's own lack of a secure identity meant that whatever his mum believed about him was the truth for him. He returned to school in a rut of despair, again balancing his need to exorcise himself of painful emotions with his desire not to be excluded. But his desire to be a part of the school, as much as we provided an oasis for him, was being eroded. He started to believe that if he was sent away – to a foster carer or a residential school – then his absence would have an effect on his mum, at least for the first few minutes of their eventual reunion. Because, he said, 'No matter how much someone hates you, after you have been away for a long time, they are always happy to see you, at least for a little while.' Eventually he started to ally his need to express painful emotions with a desire to get excluded, so that we would have to send him away.

We could no longer contain him. We had already lost two excellent teaching assistants who had both worked closely with him but left because they could not contain the despair that they felt when they were with him. Jayden left the school because of his own actions. He threatened to seriously harm another pupil, and refused to withdraw the threat. Whether this was serious or yet another attempt at getting sent away, we had no choice but to follow it up. We were determined that Jayden should go to a provision where he could be contained properly and helped to overcome his despair. But as the meetings to decide his fate moved away from our jurisdiction, the exigencies of tight budgets took over. A few months after he left us, I got a call from a post-16 college in a nearby town. It was not the one our pupils usually went to. They said that they had a pupil called Jayden coming to them, and they had heard he had a statement of special educational needs. Could we please tell them what the nature of those needs was and how we met them? Was it help with reading and writing he needed? It seemed that the college were unprepared for the shared meanings that needed to be made with Jayden, and as such he was being left to his own demons and his bleak future. What he really needed were shared meanings in which he felt valued and safe, and where adults could regulate his behaviour for him until he had learned how to do so himself. We had only provided the initial stages of such containment, and for too little time. I worried that it had not been enough for Jayden to be able to keep himself contained and safe in the future.

Part II
What does this mean for teachers? Lessons for practice

Chapter 6
How to talk to troubled children

Verbal communication evidently plays a large role in the way two people construct meanings together. This chapter details how to talk to troubled children to maximise the degree to which these meanings are shared.

Modes of talk

There are many ways in which skilled teachers work to ensure that there is the best opportunity for connection between themselves and their pupils. The behaviour of pupils who are connecting with their teacher is invariably more compliant than that of those pupils who are not, and so connection and behaviour management can be seen as synonymous.

For a teacher to have a few tricks up their sleeve to help them over any sticking points in the lesson, when behaviour or compliance is at risk of breaking down, is very useful. They can make a big difference to the course a lesson may take. For example, I was once in the hall with a group of children all aged around 10 or so, when George ran up to a display and started taking down the photos of the children who had won commendations. I told him to stop. He ignored me. I told him again, but more forcefully. He ignored me again. I moved to put my body in between him and the display, and started to prepare for the battle that would inevitably ensue, as George is a wilful young man and not averse to violence. Suddenly a teaching assistant appeared and, oblivious to my mounting frustration, said to George, 'Oh, how lovely, you are collecting pictures of your friends.' George, suddenly bereft of a force to rebel against, lost interest in the photos, handed them to the teaching assistant, and went back to the activity of the lesson, leaving me feeling rather foolish. I had very nearly allowed the situation to escalate into a fight that need not have taken place.

Here's an example of me being less foolish. One of the tricks I learned which really helped me to transform my classroom from a place of strife to one of positivity was the names on the board technique. I would write the names of the pupils on one side of the board, either before the lesson or halfway through (usually if I felt that things were getting a little out of hand). One of the pupils would invariably ask, 'Why is my name on the board?' 'Oh, it's no big deal,' I would reply, 'I just want to work out who is doing really well. I'm just going to put a tick beside everyone's name each time I see that they are doing the right thing. Right now I'm looking for people who are sitting up, sitting still and looking at me.' I'd start naming and ticking the pupils who were doing what I had just asked for. If one of them was not, I would say, 'I'll come back to you in a minute to see if I can give you that tick.' Or I would just leave them to the end of my 'survey', by which time they almost always would have realised what was needed from them. It was so much easier to manage than putting names on the board for negatives, and then trying to inflict punishments or give the child the chance to earn their break or lunchtime back, which is what I used to do.

There are other tricks of the trade too, and we will come to those in a short while. Firstly, it's important to point out that they are only 'tricks' in the sense that they are manipulative, but they need to have some heart behind them. They would be less successful if you did not already have some sort of relationship with, and regard for, the children. Secondly, such tricks are better understood if we explain the rationale behind them. So I want to present a conceptual model that encapsulates all the ways in which teachers can maintain and repair connections with their pupils. It is probably applicable for all sorts of relationships, but I am going to concentrate on how it applies in the classroom.

It is a very simple model which is easily explained. However, to fully understand any model of relationships and the behaviour management encapsulated therein you have to understand the philosophy behind it, which is where I will start. This model is based on a child-friendly approach – by which I mean that the meanings in the classroom are necessarily shared – and characterised by a genuine sense of reciprocity. Teachers do not work to impose meanings on the children but instead to lead them in an interaction which is governed by respect.

By way of contrast, there does seem to be, at the time of writing, a fashion in many schools to adopt a 'zero tolerance' approach to behaviour management. Proponents feel that very strong messages on all aspects of behaviour management (including the 'little' things like uniform and how to walk from lesson to lesson) mean that children are given the discipline and the attitude of successful people, and so their achievements will be higher. They would perhaps argue that the children choose to 'buy into' such systems, so in that sense the meanings are jointly constructed. Opponents argue that it is often harder for disadvantaged children or those with special needs to fit in with such an approach, and so they are left isolated and judged as inadequate. Therefore, it is argued, the approach is one that imposes meanings rather than generates them through consensus.

I cite these differing stances on behaviour management not to proclaim which is right and which is wrong, but simply to illustrate that there are different philosophical positions and to highlight how they differ. They differ essentially on the question of whether meanings should be imposed upon children or developed in conjunction with them. We will all have views somewhere on this spectrum, with very few of us at either extreme, I would suspect. At one end of the spectrum, where meanings are absolutely imposed on children, is indoctrination and the possibility of abuse. At the other end, where children are left to arrive at meanings by themselves, is neglect, because we live in a world where there is a great deal to learn, and that is best done through guided collaboration rather than lone discovery. Put in rather more practical terms, we can say that if collaboration means understanding and respecting boundaries, then too much emphasis on boundaries means children will feel restricted, but too little emphasis will leave children feeling adrift and anxious.

My model of how teachers connect with their learners involves an emphasis on meeting the children at least halfway. This is an approach that I have adopted out of necessity; by the time I meet them, the majority of my pupils have survived and rejected many attempts to impose meanings – in the form of protocols, manners and rules – upon them. If such attempts have ended in failure, the consequent further meanings imposed by the enforcer include blame, rejection and exclusion. Therefore, it never seemed like a good idea to adopt an authoritarian approach. As the years went by, even as I became more adept at putting boundaries in place in my classroom, I have not become more authoritarian. In fact, I have probably become less so, although my authority has increased. How is this so? The model can explain.

In this model, all teacher–pupil dialogues fit into one of four modes of interaction. These are as follows:

1. **Facilitative mode.** The teacher and the pupil work collaboratively to generate shared understandings. The relationship is asymmetrical, as the teacher is the guide, but it is also characterised by mutual respect and genuine reciprocity. This mode of interaction is important because it gives the teacher more strategies with which to guide the learner, such as the use of gentle humour. Within a positive and caring relationship, the learner may well be relaxed and secure enough to be able to laugh about some of their mistakes. Perhaps as importantly, interactions in this mode mean that goodwill is generated between the teacher and the learner. If a classroom is judged as having an insufficient quantity of facilitative talk, then adjustments to the style and content of the curriculum would have to be made so that shared meanings are more easily constructed.

2. **Authoritative mode.** There will come a time when the teacher needs to be more directive towards the pupil. Perhaps they have not got the time to explain all of the reasons why they want the learner to do something during a task. Or perhaps the pupil's behaviour is at the limits of what the teacher will accept. In authoritative mode, the teacher tells the learner to do something on the basis of the trust and respect that exists between them. The learner decides to comply because of the relationship they have with the teacher. The clearest example of this that I have in my mind is when, as a child, I would ask my mum why I had to do a particular thing, to which she would sometimes reply, 'Because I said so.' The authority for this direction comes from the relationship between the two speakers.

    However, there is a danger in this mode. Teachers who say, 'Because I said so,' too many times will eventually get learners who reply, 'And who the hell are you to tell me what to do?' or words to that effect. This is because issuing instruction in authoritative mode is cashing in on the goodwill generated in facilitative mode. Once you have run out of goodwill, you are in trouble.

3. **Authoritarian mode.** Teachers have a lot of power at their disposal in the form of disciplinary procedures, and they can, if they want, use this power to impose meaning on their pupils. But they need to beware using this technique. Often their meaning will become the dominant one, but that does not mean to say that it will be shared. Human beings have often found ways of subverting such power, and children are no different – they find ways of undermining regimes that they find too authoritarian, or of creating parallel systems in which they find it easier to gain status. Setting up gangs could be an example of such a practice. Being too authoritarian means you quickly risk precluding the chance of shared meanings being made at all.

4. **Rejection mode.** Of course, we as teachers have the power to impose one final meaning on a child if the previous three do not serve the purpose, which is to suggest that they are not worthy of inclusion in our world. If they will not, or cannot, comply, then they do not belong. If a child shares any meaning here it will damage their sense of self.

I cannot give a comprehensive list of examples of what teachers might say to demonstrate each of these modes. Obviously open-ended questions, suggestions and discussions are more likely to be facilitative, whereas 'because I said so' is more likely to be authoritative. But context, intonation and body language all play a part in helping to shape the meaning of what we say. The simple sentence, 'You do not do it like that', for example, could be used in all four modes, as the effect would be contingent on the delivery.

In my experience, good teachers spend as much time as they can in facilitative mode and as little time as possible in the other three. Shifts into authoritative or authoritarian mode need to be short and decisive, and possibly cushioned by some facilitative talk. So, for example, when Dean was walking out of the school gates, I mentioned that I would have to call the police, but then backed off so that he had nothing else to push against, and quickly changed the subject. You could try a joke if it feels appropriate. Jokes are the epitome of facilitative talk in that you cannot force someone to laugh.

Staying in facilitative mode is good for my pupils because it is the most effective way of teaching and learning but, from a more selfish point of view, is vital for me if I am to avoid burnout. In my mind I perceive my job as akin to being on a treadmill:

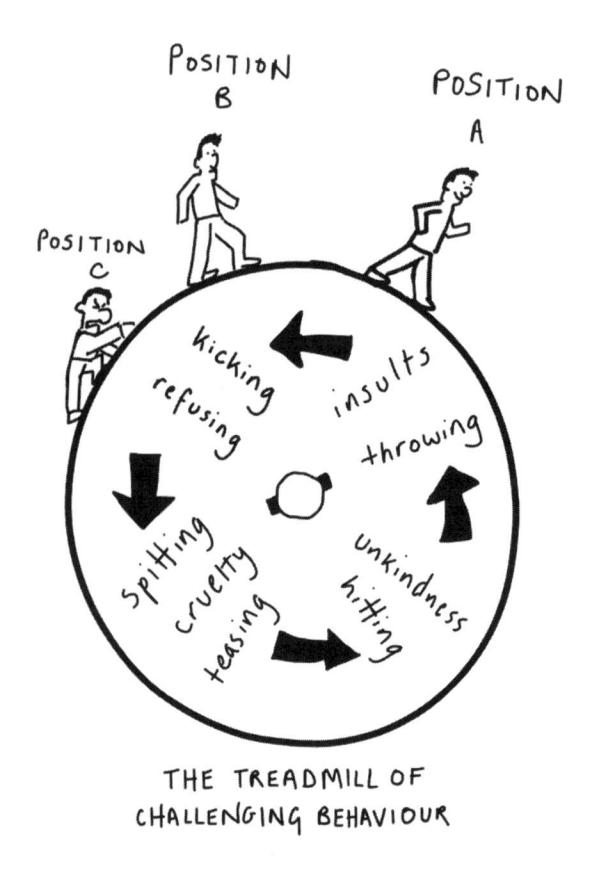

THE TREADMILL OF
CHALLENGING BEHAVIOUR

Every day, the treadmill turns, bringing new problems my way. Fights on the way to school, a lack of breakfast, a family row last night – anything can make the wheel turn faster or slower, and bring along a problem to slap me in the face. In facilitative mode, I am ahead of the game, walking confidently in position A. I can see the problems coming, the pupils have a bit of goodwill towards me that might cushion the blows somewhat, and although it is hard work, I am at least walking downhill.

But then occasionally something knocks me back to position B, and I have to work harder to get back to where I was. Fortunately, I can use my authority to repair the relationships that need attention. If I have a good, mainly facilitative, relationship with a pupil, they will act on my say-so alone, until their trust in me wears thin.

But pity the poor guy in position C. His relationships are contests, and everything is more difficult than it should be because his actions are bringing out the worst in his pupils. Desperately seeking control, he struggles not to be authoritarian. It is possible to find oneself in this position with an individual pupil, or with a whole class. It is even possible for a whole school to be in this position. As I have already mentioned, I once found myself in a school that was in rapid decline. Everything was going wrong. We were losing staff to stress, so the remaining teachers were more fractious with the pupils. The number of incidents involving restraint was rising, which meant so too were the children's anxiety levels. There was a feeling that we had to rescue the situation, so the head teacher ordered everyone into the hall and laid down the law in no uncertain terms. He was drawing a line in the sand, he said, and the next person who swore at a teacher would be gone. Within ten minutes of the assembly just such an incident occurred but the pupil did not go home, because it would not have been fair to blame all the previous crimes on this one misdemeanour. This left us worse off than before the head teacher's speech. Our failure to follow through with the sanction left everyone a little more confused, with the boundaries even less clearly demarcated. And all the time we were scrabbling to make effective authoritarian interventions, what we should really have been aiming for were more facilitative ones. But this did not seem possible. The school closed shortly after.

The art of de-escalation – tricks of the trade

Staying in facilitative mode is contingent on the teacher's individual level of skill in keeping interactions as collaborative as possible. Good teachers employ a range of strategies to keep interactions from becoming contests of will. So here is a list of some 'tricks' for getting pupils onside. These are essentially tips to avoid getting the response 'NO!'

What does this mean for teachers?

- Offer them a reward, but remember that they are probably more motivated by your recognition than the actual reward.

- Use proximal praise – don't criticise someone for slouching, praise the person beside them for sitting up straight.

- Use humour.

- Tell them to do something and then wait for them to process the thought.

- Tell them to do something and then tell them you want it done quickly, so their choice is not between doing it and not doing it, but between doing it slowly and doing it quickly.

- Tell them what you want them to do very quietly so that only they can hear and they do not 'lose face' by complying.

- Dress what you are asking them to do up as a job, so it carries more importance.

- Make sure that you are the one who sets the emotional tone, so that the conversation is calm and friendly.

- Display a list of positive behaviours on a poster and put a sealed envelope containing one of the displayed positive behaviours somewhere prominent. Make it clear that you will open the envelope at a certain time, and whoever has been demonstrating the behaviour will get a reward.

- When starting or finishing an activity, give a clearly signalled countdown. Use a timer.

- If a child is disobeying you by, say, talking to their neighbour, use the script, 'When you do …, I feel upset because …' In this way you are modelling assertive rather than aggressive communication.

- Blame inanimate or abstract structures – they are more difficult to argue with than human beings are. For example, 'The clock says it is time to start work now,' or 'I'm sorry, I would like to let you go outside for break, but the chart says that you cannot.'

- Believe that the pupil will comply.

However, this kind of thinking on your feet is only necessary when the culture and the context need some fine-tuning: it is possible to establish a facilitative classroom environment in which this dynamic becomes the norm. There are other factors, beyond face-to-face interaction, that can determine a teacher's ability to stay in facilitative mode:

- Pupils know what the teacher wants them to do.

- Pupils are able to achieve what the teacher wants them to do.

- Clear and effective structures are in place in the classroom and the playground, and personal relationships are supported, so that the child is not left to cope in a social situation that is beyond their ability.

- Lessons are planned based on accurate assessment of the pupils' academic, communicative, cognitive, social and physical needs.

- Clear expectations exist across the school around behaviour.

- Where possible, the school is engaged in a clear dialogue with the pupils about their personal development.

- Parents are involved in positive partnerships with the school.

- The school teaches the social and emotional aspects of development and learning.

- External support and/or coordinated intervention strategies are in place for those pupils for whom the usual levels of support do not suffice.

- The school follows an engaging, fun and appropriate curriculum.

The interactions between particular teachers and particular pupils are best seen within the context of the school and its ethos. No matter how good a manager of behaviour someone is, they are going to find this more difficult in a school where the pupils are feeling uncontained and are, therefore, more unruly than they would otherwise be.

Checking that you are not the problem

Being in a room with a troubled child who is in a state of crisis can be a challenging experience. If there is a charged atmosphere, or a risk of someone getting physically hurt, adrenaline can kick in. I certainly recognise that the number of factors I can focus on shrinks, and it becomes easy to forget to see what is happening from the child's point of view.

Such experiences can be draining and disorienting, even if the threat of violence does not become a reality. It is important, however, that the chaos and heightened emotions that the child is feeling do not become the decisive factors which determine the nature of the shared meanings that are constructed between teacher and pupil. It is important that the teacher is able to keep the interaction safe and productive for everyone at all times.

To ensure that the shared meaning has the characteristics which we desire, it is essential to monitor and manage our own levels of arousal. When two people are in a room together, their arousal levels will eventually match. If I am calm with an angry child, one of us is going to adapt our mood. This means that I very rarely shout or raise my voice.

This emotional matching is quite well-known, but perhaps less recognised are the other undesirable ways in which we can allow the pupils to affect the nature of the interaction. Often when dealing with troubled children, it can feel like there is a void where the usual moral or social structures should be. When I am interacting with a friend, someone whom I respect, there is a degree of mutual regulation about what constitutes acceptable talk and behaviour. With a troubled child, that lack of regulation from your interlocutor can leave one's own internal structures exposed and vulnerable. There is a risk that the adult, instead of ensuring that the shared meaning is fair and morally structured, allows what the child is bringing to the interaction – chaos, anarchy or something darker – to shape the nature of the shared meaning.

When I first started teaching, a considerable number of colleagues seemed to have internalised some of the anxieties, angers and resentments that the children were feeling. Like the children, they were using ill-advised and self-defeating behaviours. Some were acting very much like the children themselves, using 'strategies' such as:

- **Sinking to their level.** 'No, *you're* the wanker!'

- **Devaluing the experience.** This could include things like finding any excuse to avoid teaching. 'It's rained all day, so the kids haven't gone out, or had a proper break. Let's just have a pool competition this afternoon.' This is usually a vote winner with the children because they are rarely thinking long term. Furthermore, an adult who has fun like this instead of doing boring work is showing that schoolwork can't be all that important, right? Such adults were rarely the ones who the children went to for help.

- **Using the threat of physical force.** 'First I'm going to ask you nicely to do something, then I'm going to tell you. Then there will be a consequence.' This approach is particularly favoured by anyone with resentment or anger issues of their own, or anyone who feels that they have not been listened to in their life. It is a fairly draconian way of ensuring that the meanings in the classroom are the ones you want to create. Even if it is balanced by a very sensitive child-centred approach, it runs the risk of being counterproductive and can lead to a spike in the number of challenges and even restraints. If the child is cooperating out of fear, then the meaning for them in all interactions is going to be coloured by that fear and the other emotions, such as resentment, that may accompany it. This approach teaches children to be subservient rather than self-regulated, and that violence is a legitimate negotiation tool.

- **Nagging.** 'How many times do I have to tell you?' This is the rhetorical questioning of someone trying to exercise their personal authority when there is none left. The only effect of words like these is to underline the speaker's ineffectiveness. Telling someone does not mean that they have listened. Why is the adult just repeating the same behaviour over and over again? Isn't that what is irritating them about the child's behaviour? Shouldn't someone look at the bigger picture here? Nagging is, in effect, teaching a child that there are times when it is acceptable not to listen.

- **Concentrating on one's own emotions.** 'I'm sick of you doing this. You have let me down.' Putting your emotions at the fore is fine if you are modelling how to manage a successful win-win resolution to a conflict, but not if the outcome for the child is a sense of shame.

- **Using the threat of verbal bullying.** Some staff coped by becoming leaders of the pack, creating hierarchies – among both pupils and some staff – with themselves at the top. These were based on sporting prowess and occasional physical aggression, with 'banter' often the means by which status was assigned and maintained.

- **Using egocentric thinking to rationalise inappropriate actions.** A handful of staff allowed their own moral codes to slip. Perhaps believing that the stress of the job was unfair, and that they were owed something, some stole from the school as perceived recompense.

These days there is much more support, accountability and regulation than there was when I first entered the classroom. Despite this, with some staff there is still a sense of disparity between what they agree in training sessions is best practice and what they actually do. Some seem locked into styles of interaction that are self-defeating, that limit their effectiveness in creating productive shared meanings with the children. I now want to explore why this is so.

The answer lies in the fact that we adults are often no better or worse at changing our behaviours than the children are. Over my career I have worked with experts in areas such as anger management or protective behaviours, who have come into school to deliver bespoke training to individual pupils or small groups. For six weeks or so, the children receive lessons designed to target the specific problems that they are facing. The lessons are typically very good, in that I have taken ideas from them to use in my own teaching. But they have had absolutely no effect on those pupils who they were designed to help. I remember one girl not waiting to pick up her certificate of completion for the protective behaviours course, because to do so would have eaten into her break and so kept her from the boys she was so desperate to please, often in inappropriate ways.

The reason why our behaviours can be difficult to change even when we want that change is because they are a result of our thoughts and feelings, which are shaped by previous experiences. There is a link, therefore, between our behaviour and our core beliefs. Learning techniques to change our behaviour may not work if our core beliefs remain the same. So, for example, the girl who failed to benefit from the protective behaviours course possibly needed to learn to value herself more than she needed to learn which parts of her body were private or how to be assertive.

It is the same with staff. Unless they change their core beliefs about children, about teaching and learning, and often about themselves, there is probably little chance that they will put techniques for improving the shared meanings they make with pupils into effect. They will likely continue to make mistakes, such as:

- **Misattributing needs.** 'You need to sit down!' Not true. In fact, *I*, the teacher, need you, the pupil, to sit down, please.

- **Acting with righteousness.** 'You need to learn.' I once went on a course that highlighted the technique of strategic capitulation, the art of losing the odd battle so that you could win the war. The speaker pointed out that many children's school careers are jeopardised by teachers picking the wrong battle at the wrong time. I was in full agreement. The next day back at school, a very agitated boy was in my office, holding a chair above his head, ready to throw it at me. I said to him, 'You can throw that chair if you like, but then you will face the consequences. You need to learn that your behaviour back in the classroom was not acceptable.' I have since learned there are better ways of teaching and learning.

  Another form of righteousness is leaving the child to face the consequences of their actions. 'You see, I told you you'd be upset.' We need to communicate to the child that we care enough not to let them be out of control or unsafe.

- **Demonising the child.** 'He knows exactly what he's doing!' 'She's so manipulative!' 'She's just doing it because she knows she can get away with it.' This is another favourite of the righteous. While it is true that some children do deliberately undermine, disrupt or hurt, and they do know exactly what they are doing, it is important to bear in mind that they do not understand why they are doing it. They need help to learn to meet their needs through more socially acceptable behaviours.

- **Negating.** 'Don't be silly, you're usually friends, you get on fine.' 'Stop making a fuss.' 'You're so dramatic!' 'Don't be so sensitive!' This simply acts to invalidate what the child says they are feeling. In using negation, you are denying rather than sharing in their meaning.

- **Shaming.** 'How old are you? Don't you think you should act your age?' Do you really think this line of questioning will get you anywhere?

- **Blaming.** 'You knew exactly what you were doing – it was your fault.' It may be tempting to explain failure by employing judgement or blame. The pupil is being stupid, unfair, disobedient or hurtful, and they are breaking the rules. This may be true from your point of view, of course, but from the pupil's perspective, there will be another interpretation. Once you have made everyone safe it is your job to try to work out the meaning behind their actions. You cannot do that if you have written them off.

    Of course, you may not choose to blame the pupil. You can blame their parents or the culture that they have been brought up in. You could blame the management of the school, who in turn could blame the local authority. 'We told them this kid would be trouble, and that we needed more bodies in the classroom for support, so no wonder things have gone this badly.'

- **Perpetuating myths.** Another tempting way to fill the void is to reach for a myth. 'Oh, he's just like his brother/father/mother!' It's a nice way of avoiding engaging with a problem and the feelings that are tangled up in it. So discount anyone who tells you myths about children being cruel, boys being boys, brothers always fighting sisters, boys liking guns, or girls fighting meaner than boys. What the pupil needs is for you to help them by working out why they are behaving in such a way, not to be dismissed as the embodiment of a stereotype. Another popular diversion is to reach for the medical card and talk of diagnoses and drug dosages. It's important not to give up doing what you can for the child, and not leave it to the doctors, even if 'he's got that ADHD'.

- **Focusing on internalised shame.** Here there is no external speech, just an anger towards the pupil who, you feel, is making you feel shame because you do not seem to be able to manage this pupil as well as other colleagues do.

This is another example of focusing on your own feelings rather than those of the child in the interaction.

- **Needing to deny.** 'Yes, he spat in my face, but that's alright. He was upset, so I understand.' Removing boundaries makes everyone feel unsafe. There is another form of denial, which is simply being poor at listening to children or noticing their needs.

- **Needing to discharge.** 'I can't believe you just did that, what on earth is wrong with you?' You may seek to discharge painful emotions through shouting or otherwise expressing anger.

- **Believing that play is different to learning.** 'If only you'd pay as much attention to your work as you do to that game.' Some people seem to have a core belief that learning is always a serious matter. They do not realise that, for children, one of the prime motivators for play is the learning they get from it.

I have made many of these mistakes along the way, and I continue to refine my approach. It is important for staff to be able to revise their core beliefs and their behaviours. If they do not, why should the children?

How to avoid the traps

Monitoring your own language for these sorts of mistakes is helpful, but even better is to start developing a checklist for positive behaviours.

Here's a quick list of questions to ask yourself to check that you are managing the situation for yourself and for the pupils:

- Am I fighting the right battle?

- Am I in control?

- Am I staying balanced?

- What emotions am I feeling? (It's likely that they are feeling the same way.)

- What is this behaviour telling me about the child's thoughts, feelings and long-term needs?
- Can I model emotional strength?
- What do I need to do in the short term to help this child return to a more positive state of mind?
- Can I show them a better way of resolving this issue now, or should I leave that until later?
- What boundaries or support can I put in to make this situation safe, and to make the pupil feel calm and contained?
- How can I facilitate their return to normal school life? Will they need help with any reconciliations or apologies?
- Could we have prevented this?

There is a very fine but clear distinction between ensuring that you are the person who determines the quality of shared meanings and imposing your own meaning on the child. After there has been an incident of challenging behaviour, for example, there is still the need for a jointly constructed dialogue. This is rarely achieved by the traditional teacher reaction to challenging behaviour, which is the telling off. It may be important for the teacher to reassert a sense of hierarchy:

Do I make myself clear?

Yes.

Yes what?

Yes, Sir.

However, the problem I have with telling off is that it allows the pupil an easy way out. Keep your head down, mumble a few platitudes, say sorry when you are told to, and the job is done. The telling off may work as a deterrent for repeating whatever behaviour was the problem, but if so, it will be as a result of increased obedience rather than self-regulation.

After a crisis, by which I mean a breakdown in communication of any size in which the emotions have been called into play, there is a golden opportunity for emotional growth. The pupil's world view has not only been found to be ineffective, but their emotions are all up in the air, and perhaps they will be open to prompting to change their ways. That is going to be achieved through the development of (perhaps new) shared meanings, not the imposition of the teacher's view upon the pupil. Yes, the school has rules which need to be reasserted, and boundaries have been broken, but we are there to teach the child, not just to maintain order. We are teachers, not the police.

Teaching to the gaps

Of course, we should not just teach children the skills they need after an incident has highlighted the gap in their repertoire. We need to be more proactive than that. The child who bullies, for example, is using aggression to get what they want, be it a sense of control or importance, or to pass the fear that they themselves are feeling on to someone else. Teaching them to express themselves assertively rather than aggressively is vital, therefore. In my experience, bullies are often scared and find it difficult to express themselves assertively.

I mentioned before how the courses on anger management and protective behaviours that I witnessed were almost wholly ineffective, so I need to explain why I am recommending such interventions now. Those courses were delivered in a somewhat generic way, as the presenters did not really know the children. They used hypothetical examples, which meant that the children had to be able to extrapolate and generalise from them: an ability which they typically lacked. If such lessons are not confined to a six-week burst, but are instead threaded throughout the curriculum, and are delivered by teachers who know the pupils very well and can teach by using examples from their own lives, then there is a much greater chance of success.

There are many such skills which troubled children need to learn, and some excellent models out there for teaching them – for example, The SCERTS Model.[1] Here is a quick summary of what I would deem essential topics and skills on the troubled child's curriculum:

- **Developing a voice.** Knowing the difference between aggressive talk (which makes things worse), wimpy talk (which changes nothing) and assertive talk (which is the best way to get you what you want).

- **Listening skills.** Body posture, eye contact, allowing the other person time to speak, asking questions, reflecting back, showing empathy and avoiding conversation killers (such as changing the subject or offering judgements).

- **Managing the emotions.** Naming emotions, recognising them in oneself and in others, developing empathy, anger management, anxiety management and understanding mental health.

- **Practising how to talk.** Turn-taking, small talk, asking questions and sharing the subject.

- **Conflict resolution.** Listening, reflecting back, compromising and finding win-win solutions.

All these skills can be built into the curriculum as well as taught discretely. Planning projects in design and technology, for example, could be a way of developing empathy, as the needs of the users of the end product have to be taken into account. In maths, role play activities around giving and receiving the correct change could be designed to incorporate assertive rather than aggressive communication. There are many ways in which we can adapt the curriculum to allow all these skills to be taught.

---

1 Barry M. Prizant, Amy M. Wetherby, Emily Rubin, Amy C. Laurent and Patrick J. Rydell, *The SCERTS Model: Comprehensive Educational Approach for Children with Autism Spectrum Disorders* (Baltimore, MD: Paul Brookes Publishing, 2006).

Chapter 7
Self-regulation and supportive interventions

My journey from the chaos of my early days as a teacher of troubled children through to developing the understandings I have explored so far in this book leads here, to a theoretical model of the interplay between the emotions and learning. Despite the variety of the behaviours I have encountered, it is possible to come up with a theoretical explanation that applies to all children – from those, like Millie, who are so anxious they are scared to take part in any shared meanings to ones, like Imelda, who try to completely fill the space between themselves and others with their own words, or, like Martha, have to ensure they take control of the whole process. We have seen a number of ways in which children's emotions hinder the creation of shared meanings, but we have seen that we adults can play our part too. We can put our needs before the child's, or we can fail to ensure that these meanings feel reciprocal, safe, accepting and hopeful.

Perhaps the easiest way to construct this knowledge into a theoretical model is to consider in greater detail the effect of shared meanings on the learner, who, after all, should be the primary focus. The dialogue of constructing shared meanings becomes internalised by the learner to enhance their own mental monologue, and their way of making sense of the world and their capacity to impact upon it. I start off this chapter with an exploration of the internal monologue, as understanding it helps to make clear the role of the emotions in teaching and learning.

The role of the internal monologue

The monologue inside our heads is the vehicle we use to think with, make decisions and act. As was demonstrated in Chapter 1, the learner's internal monologue is constructed and reshaped through dialogue with others. Our internal monologues incorporate our feelings as well as our thoughts. Our feelings motivate us to use our thinking to make sense of the world. And when our thoughts prove inadequate, the emotions take over. In formal teaching and learning, the ideal would be that any gaps in the learner's internal monologue are temporarily bridged by the dialogue with the teacher in such a way that the learner can appropriate new ways of thinking and feeling to overcome the gaps and engage with new skills and understandings. Once the learner has internalised this dialogue for themselves, they have a greater capacity for self-regulation. Their internal monologue becomes sufficiently robust for them to take on a new task or think through a new concept by themselves.

The concept of the internal monologue is quite simple, but the reality of it is complex because how a person thinks and feels is a result of the unique set of experiences, feelings and thoughts that they have had to date. We cannot assume that our words can be planted in the learner's head with ease. For example, if two pupils are playing pool and one gets angry at the other's perceived cheating, I cannot stand behind the aggrieved pupil, say out loud what I would like them to think and expect them to think it. I may want to provide a model for a successful resolution to the problem by saying something like, 'Okay, that is annoying, but we must remember to keep calm, breathe and remember the bigger picture. We should aim to be assertive rather than aggressive.' But the pupil may be thinking: 'He's bloody cheated again! Sod him, I'm sick of him, and I kind of know that I should be listening to Mr Nelmes, but actually, right at this moment, I just want to hit him too to make him shut up!'

It is important to recognise, therefore, that we cannot easily rewrite children's internal monologues for them. Sometimes this internal monologue can be nigh on impossible to change. Jayden, mentioned multiple times, often went into a kind of crisis mode, in which he would be overcome by strong feelings and difficult thoughts, expressed in the form of challenging behaviour. At such times he was seemingly impervious to any advice we gave him. He would say afterwards that we should have reminded him about the strategies for coping with upset that we had all agreed upon when he was calm and willing to engage. This advice included going to the quiet room and taking five deep breaths. We were flabbergasted – had he not heard us repeating this very advice to him throughout the incident? Clearly not. The problem was that on a 10-point anxiety scale, Jayden did not seem to have the numbers 2 through 8. He shot right up to the far end of the scale as soon as his anxiety was triggered, leaping past the point at which he could use the rational voice in his internal monologue to manage the difficulties he was facing. His way of feeling emotions had been shaped by previous experience. Perhaps some of these reaction patterns were set up when he had little or no language with which to frame the traumatic situations he found himself in, and so it remains difficult for him to use language and cognition as coping tools when life becomes hard – when he is confronted by the many situations for which his internal monologue is not yet robust or resilient enough to be of help.

In our discussion of the internal monologue as a means of self-regulation, it is important to bear in mind two things. Firstly, the internal monologue channels both our thoughts and our emotions. Secondly, the pattern of interplay between these two elements in an individual may well be as unique as their fingerprints. Because this internal monologue is linked to the emotions and is shaped by our experiences, we need to recognise that some of the forces which have shaped its nature may be deep-rooted and hidden from view. Unless the learner has the capacity – in terms of their emotional disposition – for taking ownership of the meaning that the teacher is making, no learning will occur. For example, I saw a teacher trying very sensitively but assertively to reassure one girl in the class that all the adults were rooting for her, telling her that if she had any problems, all she had to do was come to the teacher or teaching assistants and they would always help, so there was no need for the outbursts of physical and verbal aggression that she was displaying. The teacher did her best to contain the pupil by reassuring her and seeking to help her develop better strategies for coping with difficult emotions. Unfortunately, I fear that this teacher's attempts were in vain. The pupil in question has a degenerative disease that is slowly but surely taking away her ability to speak and walk. This is a problem that, no matter how hard they work or want to help, the adults in the class can do nothing about. The pupil knows this and will therefore, I suspect, not easily buy into the teacher's message that everything will be all right if she seeks help.

The nature of self-regulation

The quality of our internal monologue determines the extent to which we can regulate our own behaviour. The more complete and robust our internal monologue, the greater our capacity for self-regulation, and our ability to cope. Different people will have different levels of self-regulation, and, of course, the same person can have different levels in different tasks. Some elements of self-regulation are specific to particular tasks, whereas others are more general. When we learn how to do a task, we also learn about learning in general, and develop skills and knowledge that are applicable to other situations.

Now let us look at self-regulation and the internal monologue in more detail in order to understand the role of the emotions in teaching and learning more fully. The rest of this chapter explores three aspects of this issue:

- The components of self-regulation.
- The role of context in the creation of the internal monologue.
- How to support the internal monologue of the troubled learner.

The components of self-regulation

If the teaching has been successful, the teacher will have passed on enough knowledge for the learner to complete a task unaided. If we break down the skills that are involved in most tasks, we can see that self-regulation involves the ability to manage and direct our internal monologue on both the cognitive and emotional level. As Graham, Harris and Reid suggest, we need to be able to direct our attention to the salient aspects of the subject under focus.[1] We need to be creative in our invention of solutions, but be able to maintain focus and keep our criteria for success clear. We need to be able to access our memory, and be able to plan and execute our next steps in a measured way. At the same time, we need to be able to cope with anxieties linked to the possibility of failure, and what that

---

1   Steve Graham, Karen R. Harris and Robert Reid, Developing Self-Regulated Learners. *Focus on Exceptional Children*, 24(6) (1992): 1–16.

might mean for our self-image. We need to be able to reassure ourselves and control invasive impulses or desires.

These abilities can be drawn on at a conscious or unconscious level, and clearly involve the emotions and cognition in a transactional relationship. For example, the more something makes sense, the more the learner can use their powers of reasoning and the less they will have to direct their energy into coping with emotions such as anxiety around the task. The more unsure or nervous the learner is, the more difficult it will be for them to think clearly, because their energies are being directed towards the emotional components of the task.

The internal monologue has to be complete and robust enough to guide the learner's thinking and feeling in such a way that they can complete the task. If there are gaps or weaknesses, then the learner will fail, unless the teacher can spot the gap and provide the appropriate support at the right time. For example, if the learner is not defining the problem correctly – i.e. not asking themselves what they have to do to approach the problem constructively – the teacher has to encourage them to do so, perhaps through dialogue first. Similarly, if the learner has a tendency to let negative thoughts and emotions creep in when an error is made, the teacher has to model a form of self-reinforcement and resilience that the learner can adopt for themselves. Even completing the task successfully may bring on its own anxieties, and the teacher may have to model how to accept being successful. A number of my learners would not be thinking what may seem obvious – for example, 'I'm really proud of this!' They may be struggling with less comfortable thoughts and feelings such as, 'I hate it when people judge me, and this is probably rubbish anyway.' When any strategy falters, the learner's only hope is a teacher who can fill the gap for them, despite any challenging behaviours the learner may be exhibiting.

The role of context in the creation of the internal monologue

We can add another layer of complexity to our consideration, another way in which the emotions can impinge on the learning process. The process of self-regulation does not take place in a vacuum. Lessons and learning take place in a physical environment – in schools or other institutions – in which there is a dominant ethos and belief system, and other people to which the learner relates in a certain way. Graham, Harris and Reid give the example of a pupil who is learning to improve their writing.[2] As part of their self-regulatory strategies, they might think about how the teacher will react to their work, and seek their praise.

With the children I have taught, the picture can be more complex. For example, getting praise cannot always be assumed to be motivating. Even in many of the mainstream schools I have been in, there are children whose sources of motivation do not fit neatly within the dominant discourse of the institution. These children may have had experiences which led them to hold other beliefs about the work they are asked to do. So, when they are given a writing task, for example, their goal may be somewhat different to the one that underpins our list of strategies. Perhaps, in the past, they have tried and failed to get praise from the teacher several times, and so they have learned to look elsewhere for recognition or validation. Perhaps the identity of non-achiever brings them more kudos, at least among their classmates. For many of my pupils, visible achievement left them vulnerable to criticism from their peers. In my schooldays, the epithet of choice was 'swot'. Later it became 'boff'. So a pupil's goal, therefore, may actually be to avoid visible success and the consequent praise from the teacher, because that would lead to a loss of status among similarly disaffected friends. We have to be aware that other agendas might be at play in our classrooms. It can help if we ask ourselves, 'What does it actually mean to the learner to be sitting working in the classroom?'

---

2 Graham, Harris and Reid, Developing Self-Regulated Learners.

Winkley presents a useful list of factors which affect a learner's sense of self within the classroom:[3]

- The sense of being safe, of physical and emotional security.

- The sense of intrinsic worth and being valued for oneself.

- A sense of identity, the feeling of having a sense of self in relation to other activities and to the activities of daily living.

- A sense of affiliation, the feeling of belonging and being linked to others.

- A sense of competence; a feeling of empowerment and being able to cope with life.

- A sense of mission; having a sense of what one wants to achieve.

If we put this in terms of the internal monologue, the following questions are just some of those that may be swilling around the mind of the learner on a conscious or unconscious level:

- Can I trust the person who is telling me what to do?

- If I succeed, will that bring further challenges?

- Is there a risk of failure or ridicule? What are the implications of either?

- What is my past experience? Is there any reason not to think that this activity will just repeat an old pattern?

- Do I want to align myself with the teacher and their views? Are there other people who I would rather impress or align myself with?

- Is it safe to try to take this task on?

- Do I know where my life is going? How will engaging in this activity help?

So we would hope that all our children feel safe, valued and a recognised part of the community – a community in which their achievements are celebrated and

---

3   Linda Winkley, *Emotional Problems in Children and Young People* (London and New York: Cassell, 1996).

they can feel a burgeoning sense of competence and maturation – all of which will encourage exciting thoughts about their future. But for the child with EBD, things are usually very different.

For many of the children I have taught, classrooms are strange territories, where often there is no agenda other than to avoid experiences that further damage or shame – such as with Dean, who we met back in Chapter 1 – or that draw attention to the gap between their internal world and the world of education and future employability. Learning involves change, and that in itself can make a pupil feel unsafe, as seemed to be the case with Phil (as explored in Chapter 1). Often the pupil feels no sense of belonging. If they do settle into school, they know that the feeling is temporary, or that it is ultimately unable to change the horrors of their own reality (as we saw with Maizzie in Chapter 3), or that the school is a little Arcadia that one can inhabit for a few years before the inevitable return to the big wide world out there, where survival is probably impossible (as it seemed for Jayden, who we've met several times).

How to support the internal monologue of the troubled learner

There is one final layer of complexity to explore. I have already talked about the necessity of helping children to identify and manage their unmet needs, and understanding the internal monologue gives us the structure and detail to show how that can be done. We need to aim to be in facilitative mode – rather than authoritative, authoritarian or rejection mode – as much as we can. We need to refine these concepts a little for children who are troubled.

At the start of this book I stated that there are some essential differences when it comes to teaching troubled learners. I mentioned that I have to play several roles – such as that of counsellor – as well as being a teacher. I also mentioned that sometimes I have to interpret both words and actions, and there are times when I have to take control of the whole of the interaction. On occasion, I have to stand in the way of certain courses of action or lines of thought, and guide the pupil in a hopefully more productive direction. The modes of teacher–pupil dialogue that

I have outlined – facilitative, authoritative, authoritarian and rejection – are comprehensive in that they cover the talk of teaching, but we need to extend them if we are to cover the interactions in which the teacher is trying to help a child get to the point where shared meanings – i.e. learning – can start to happen.

As I have said, there are ethical issues to consider here. I came up against some of them in practice initially. For example, having been a pupil myself at a school whose ethos included fear, corporal punishment and no small amount of abuse, I was determined to be the kind of teacher who avoided anything resembling this. But I remember what I felt the first time I made a pupil break down in tears: it was relief. I had not set out to be unkind or harsh, and when the pupil eventually started crying, I, of course, comforted them, was sorry that they had got upset, and resolved to be a bit gentler the next time. But my predominant feeling was relief that the antisocial behaviour that they had been relentlessly pursuing would now cease, and we could move forward.

How can we ensure that such moments are indeed ethical? How can we be sure that the actions of the teacher are designed to meet the pupil's needs and not the teacher's own? There are two main ways, it seems to me, in which we can ensure that such interventions are respectful to the child. Firstly, we need to work to create an environment of openness and accountability. All but the first two settings that I have worked in have been extremely supportive, warm and positive. They have to be in order to counteract the sadness and the anger that many of the children bring into the classroom. Our interventions have to counterbalance this negativity. Children come to units like ours from mainstream schools, hurt by rejection, frightened, wary and expecting this new episode in their lives to be the same as the others: damaging to their identity and self-worth, and yet more proof that they are unworthy. If all this is recognised, and counteracting these negative preconceptions becomes an important part of the ethos, then there is little or no room for individual teachers (consciously or unconsciously) to pursue agendas that do not have the children's best interests at heart.

The second way in which to ensure that our actions are ethical is to reference them against a theoretical framework, such as the one provided for professional counsellors. This is actually very applicable, if we recognise that for many teachers the job entails counselling as well as teaching. The counselling model recognises my suggested ways of getting a child ready to start making the shared meanings that constitute teaching and learning. Heron, for example, categorises counselling interventions thus:[4]

Authoritative interventions

- Prescriptive – directing the behaviour of the client.

- Informative – imparting knowledge or information to the client.

- Confronting – raising the client's consciousness about some limiting attitude or behaviour of which they are relatively unaware.

Facilitative interventions

- Cathartic – enabling the client to discharge painful emotions.

- Catalytic – eliciting self-discovery, self-directed learning and problem-solving in the client.

- Supportive – affirming the self-worth and value of the client's person, qualities, attitudes or actions.

This is the work that teachers seem to spend most of their energies on, and yet it often goes unrecognised. Our outlook needs to change at a systemic level. For example, I have met school inspectors who espouse the rather simplistic doctrine that all behaviour problems can be solved by effective classroom management. This is reductive thinking which fails to recognise the degree of trauma that some children face in their lives, and the amount of work professionals have to put in to try to counteract this damage.

It all boils down to this

We have seen how the process of creating shared meanings – and, by extension, the process of teaching and learning – has three dimensions:

---

4   John Heron, *Helping the Client: A Creative Practical Guide*, 5th edn (London: Sage, 2001).

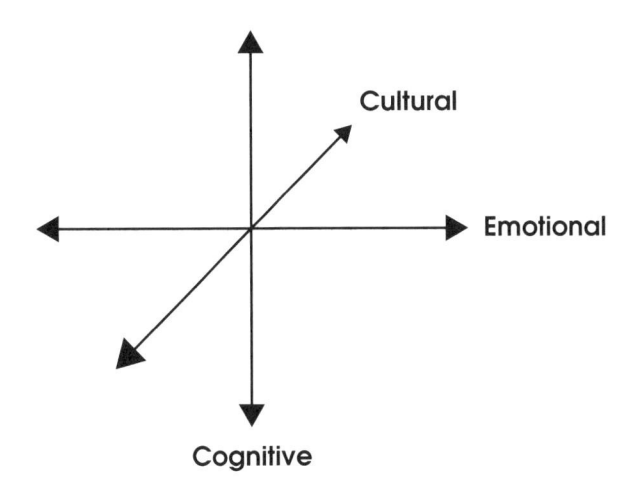

The three dimensions of teaching and learning

When teachers plan to connect with a learner, they have to be cognisant of that learner's academic or cognitive level. If they pitch their lesson too high, the content will not make any sense. Too low, and nothing gets learned. Moreover, teachers have to be cognisant that their actions and speech will be culturally specific. The milestones of cognitive development are universal, but they are reached by paths that are specific to the learner's socio-historical context. Our language, actions and our beliefs are shaped at least in part by the culture in which we live. Teachers have to teach in a way that recognises and respects the cultural diversity of their learners, because not to do so would be to hinder the richness of the shared meanings they can create in the classroom. They need to ensure the language they use is accessible to all their learners, and does not disadvantage anyone whose own language practices may be different because of their ethnicity, gender, religious beliefs and so on.

We need to recognise that the same recognition and respect has to be extended to the emotional developmental levels of the learners in our classrooms. We need to acknowledge that there is a transactional relationship between cognitive and emotional development. The central argument of this book is that each child is also at a specific level of emotional development, which needs to be acknowledged in the classroom too. For children with significant emotional difficulties, this can play such a significant role that, unless the teacher is able to understand and help them to manage their emotional state, virtually all chance of learning is gone. Not only that, but because we have put the child in a situation of deficit, they cannot help but start to internalise that deficit into their view of themselves as a learner.

The good news is that if we pitch our lessons with regard to these three dimensions – and ensure that the content and delivery of the lesson is commensurate with the cognitive, cultural and emotional needs of the child – we won't have to manage behaviour problems, as the child will have no unmet needs. The bad news is that we have to recognise that, by the same token, all behaviour problems are a result of the disparity between the child's needs and the style and content of the lesson.

Checking the emotional dimension of teaching and learning means asking questions such as:

- Does the lesson demand an ability to empathise, or to see multiple perspectives, which the learner does not yet have?

- Does the lesson demand an ability to interact with others that the learner does not yet possess, either because of underdeveloped social skills, unhealthy interaction patterns due to past trauma, and/or attachment difficulties?

- Does the lesson underestimate the levels of anxiety, anger or sadness which the learner is experiencing, and which will impact on their ability to take part in creating shared meanings?

- Does the lesson fit in with the learner's desires and motivations?

- Does the learner feel safe in the lesson?

- Does the lesson build up or erode the learner's sense of self?

Of course, the emotional dimension is not separate from the other two. There is a transactional dynamic at play here: if you are creating a genuine shared meaning with a pupil, there will be teaching and learning happening in both the cognitive and the emotional dimension. Considering all that I have said, it may seem that lesson planning is incredibly complex. But, luckily, this is not the case; if the pupil is happy to engage with the teacher and the lesson, then there is a very good chance that the lesson ticks all the right boxes.

For many pupils whose stories I have told in this book, perhaps the perfect curriculum would be, at least at the start, in the form of one-to-one support by someone who can sensitively attune to their needs and work precisely at their level of cognitive and emotional development in a safe environment that builds trust. For some, the emphasis would be on recreating opportunities for early play experiences. For others, the emphasis would be on giving time and space to heal wounds in a restorative environment. Others would be allowed to follow the few interests that remained open to them after disaffection had closed down the more traditional routes of learning.

Phil, for example, would have learned how to create shared meanings by taking part in activities that were physical, outside and involving working with animals. Jayden would have found a place where his value was recognised and his difficult feelings were identified, respected and worked through. Not everyone has a great talent, but we all have our interests and passions. For Millie it was art, while Martha loved music and dance. These interests are like islands in a swamp, the only place where the base of a bridge from and to the outside world could possibly be situated. And all the time, the curriculum would be creating opportunities for emotional development: for learning what emotions feel like, what their names are, how to manage them, how to recognise them in others, how they guide us in our actions, and how they help us decide what kind of world we want to live in. Most of the emotions felt by the pupils in response to the curriculum would, of course, be positive ones: excitement, togetherness, pride and hope. The lessons would be characterised by facilitative talk – a new experience for many troubled children – which would lead to validation of the children as people who are on the same journey as everyone else, not rejection of them as inhabitants of a world set apart.

Oh, and behaviour management techniques would be largely redundant.

Conclusion

We are all troubled

In the introduction I mentioned the objections I have to the labels that are put on troubled children. They are unfair because they infer that the locus of the problem is the child. Being sad is not the problem, whatever causes the sadness is. Another objection I have to the labelling process is the impression of 'us' and 'them' that it casts. The suggestion seems to be that those children have difficulties with their emotions and their behaviour, whereas the rest of us do not.

To have no emotional difficulties, a person would have to know exactly who they are even in the face of the existential dilemmas that being human involves. Or they would have to live a life so well-organised that they never encounter situations that would cause a level of anxiety which outstrips the resources they routinely use to cope. Claiming to live in either of these ways would indicate such a level of self-deception that it would be seen as a form of madness. All of us experience times when life is hard, and when we struggle to feel that we have any control.

Even when the rest of us – who proceed through this life without any label of special educational need – feel in control, do we have no behaviour problems? Do we always make sensible choices? Are all our decisions rational, and never undermined by our deeper desires? Of course we adults get things as wrong as our children do. We can pursue the wrong goals, try to use shortcuts to happiness which turn out to be more harmful than helpful, and engage in self-destructive practices. We can lose the ability to connect with others or with the world. We can remain egocentric and infantile. Tantrums, outbursts of petty jealousy, squabbling and more serious acts of abuse and aggression are not the sole preserve of troubled children.

We need to acknowledge that being troubled is part of the human condition. We grow by learning, by finding out about the world, about ourselves and how we fit together. It is hopefully a natural feeling to want to keep exploring, to never find enough answers to want to stop looking for more. Each peak climbed gives you a view of the next one on the path. And if the peak was really easy to summit, and caused you no anxiety, then perhaps you really do need to follow a more challenging path if you want to find out all that life has to offer.

I have learned from working with troubled children that on life's journey there is a transactional relationship between self-knowledge and knowledge of the world. We discover both forms of knowledge through connection with others. Learning gives you more than just knowledge of the world; it gives you knowledge of yourself too. The same is true of teaching. To teach or to learn – or to truly find yourself – you have to increase your connection to others and resist the temptation to turn inward too much. We usually work best when connected with others.

Once when I was suffering from anxiety after the death of my father, and in the face of problems at work, my wife said that she knew that my problems were big and all, but what happened to being a husband and a father? It was the best thing anyone could have asked of me, because it was in trying to fulfil those roles that I found myself again. I realise that if I had not had the resources to redirect my energies at the time, my wife's outburst could have added to my problems. But she judged it right, and her actions underlined an important point, which is that although we often see the endpoint of children's maturation and learning as independence, what we really mean is that we want them to become independently interdependent, with the ability to see how they fit into the social fabric of our shared existence. The pinnacle of learning is not self-sufficiency, but an increased ability to be of help to others. We help ourselves by helping others, and vice versa. That is why in my classrooms I display the words attributed to the Dalai Lama: 'Be kind whenever possible. It is always possible.' It is there for the adults as much as for the children. Is it possible to have a kinder education system? I would like to hope so.

In conclusion, let us return for one final look at the components of the classroom interaction: the learner, the teacher and the context. My central argument is that the presence of behaviour problems – by which I mean anything from opting out of the dialogue to throwing chairs – should trigger the teacher's desire to change the transactional relationship between these components.

Given the understandings of challenging behaviour that we now have, I want to address once more the concept of shame that dogs these children. It is shaming to have been the victim, and perhaps later the perpetrator, of aggression or abuse. It is shaming to spend so long in school and yet be largely unsuccessful at learning – to be 18 years old with the reading age of a primary schoolchild, for example. This book argues that some of that shame is ours, and that we must recognise and take ownership of it. Our current system usually only identifies emotional difficulties in children once their behaviour has become challenging, and we have limited ways of responding to these difficulties. All too often we use punishments or exclusions. We argue that we only have a finite amount of resources, so we cannot change, as our hands are tied by the school and the system; it should be the child that changes. This needs to stop. If behaviour seems to necessitate the use of punishment, this should trigger the recognition that change is needed in the relationship between the teacher, the learner and the context. That change is best effected by the managers of the relationship – and cannot simply be enforced upon the other players in the dynamic; it must be enacted inwardly too.

We therefore need more teachers who have the capacity to understand what challenging behaviour is communicating, as well as the capacity to deal with it in a constructive way. But, actually, this is not sufficient. It should not be down to individual teachers to simply give more of themselves. We need to have a policy level response in which there is recognition that challenging behaviour is a sign that we have got things wrong, that we have failed to assess and respond to the learner's emotional development, and that our assessment tools and the provision for helping these learners need to be reviewed. We want to empower these vulnerable children, but true empowerment only comes from working *with* the disadvantaged, not *for* them or *on* them. In other words, we need to be able to create shared meanings that are based on mutual acceptance and respect, and which involve equal levels of collaboration.

This book shows that this is possible, even though it may, at times, be difficult and may even involve a leap of faith. To continue with systems which meet challenging behaviour with the impositions of external judgements rather than interpretations of the true meanings for the children themselves would mean that we not only fail to help some of the most vulnerable children in our schools, but we reinforce their vulnerability by leaving them with a choice between two undesirable options. They can either choose to go elsewhere for their affirmation or they can internalise the disapproval they are shown and damage further their already precarious sense of self. If we accept that emotional factors can play as large a role in learning as cognitive factors can, then we can adapt our practice to take account of these differences. We can stop reinforcing the process, which, in finding troubled children in deficit, further hampers their potential for learning. Of all the forms of shame I have mentioned, this is the biggest issue for us all. Troubled children need our faith in them.

Bibliography

Bruner, Jerome (1985). Vygotsky: A Historical and Conceptual Perspective. In James V. Wertsch (ed.), *Culture, Communication, and Cognition: Vygotskian Perspectives* (Cambridge: Cambridge University Press), pp. 21–34.

Cooper, Paul, Colin J. Smith and Graham Upton (1994). *Emotional and Behavioural Difficulties: Theory to Practice* (Abingdon and New York: Routledge).

Department of Education and Department for Health (2015). *Special Educational Needs and Disability Code of Practice: 0 to 25 Years – Statutory Guidance for Organisations Which Work with and Support Children and Young People Who Have Special Educational Needs or Disabilities*. Ref: DFE-00205-2013 (January). Available at: https://www.gov.uk/government/publications/send-code-of-practice-0-to-25.

Edelsky, Carole (1991). *With Literacy and Justice for All* (London: Falmer).

Graham, Steve, Karen R. Harris and Robert Reid (1992). Developing Self-Regulated Learners. *Focus on Exceptional Children*, 24(6): 1–16.

Heron, John (2001). *Helping the Client: A Creative Practical Guide*, 5th edn (London: Sage).

Maslow, Abraham H. (1943). A Theory of Human Motivation. *Psychological Review*, 50(4): 370–396.

Mercer, Neil (1993). *The Guided Construction of Knowledge: Talk Amongst Teachers and Learners* (Bristol: Multilingual Matters).

Miller, Alice (1983). *For Your Own Good: The Roots of Violence in Child-rearing* (London: Virago Press).

Prizant, Barry M. with Tom Fields-Meyer (2016). *Uniquely Human: A Different Way of Seeing Autism* (New York: Simon & Schuster).

Prizant, Barry M., Amy M. Wetherby, Emily Rubin, Amy C. Laurent and Patrick J. Rydell (2006). *The SCERTS Model: Comprehensive Educational Approach for Children with Autism Spectrum Disorders* (Baltimore, MD: Paul Brookes Publishing).

Sinason, Valerie (2010). *Mental Handicap and the Human Condition: An Analytic Approach to Intellectual Disability*, 2nd edn (London: Free Association Books).

Winkley, Linda (1996). *Emotional Problems in Children and Young People* (London and New York: Cassell).